KU-257-096

CONTENTS

SECTION A: THE PRACTICE OF LEARNER-MANAGED LEARNING

SECTION B: THEORETICAL ISSUES AND PRACTICAL IMPLICATIONS

SECTION C: POLICY ISSUES

LIST OF CONTRIBUTORS

Professor Betty ANDERSON	is Dean and Head of the Faculty of Health at the University of Western Sydney Macarthur, Australia
Professor David BOUD	is Head of the School of Adult and Language Education at the University of Technology, Sydney, Australia
Professor Tyrrell BURGESS	is Professor of the Philosophy of Social Institutions at the University of East London, United Kingdom
Professor Len CAIRNS	is Professor and Head of the School of Education at Monash University College Gippsland, Australia
Richard DOBES	is a Director of INVENTA, Executive Development and Management Consultancy, Prague, Czechoslovakia
Ginny ELEY	is an Educational Consultant based at Bishops Stortford, United Kingdom
Norman EVANS	is Director of the Learning From Experience Trust based in United Kingdom
Dr Bertie EVERARD	is an Educational Consultant working with the Development Training Advisory Group and based in Welwyn Garden City, United Kingdom
Professor Gerry FOWLER	was Rector of the Polytechnic of East London (now the University of East London), United Kingdom
Professor Norman GRAVES	was Pro-Director (Professional Studies) at the Institute of Education, University of London, United Kingdom
Dr Jane HENRY	is Tutor at the Institute of Educational Technology, Open University, United Kingdom
Dr Joy HIGGS	is Head of the School of Physiotherapy in the Faculty of Health Sciences, University of Sydney, Australia

Eunice HINDS   is Director of the College for Independent
                                   Study, Oxford, United Kingdom

Dr Cathy HULL   is Lecturer in Experiential Learning at
                                   Goldsmith College, University of London,
                                   United Kingdom

Mike LAYCOCK   is Programme Director of the Enterprise Unit
                                   at the University of East London, United
                                   Kingdom

Professor Diane MONTGOMERY   is Dean of the Faculty of Education and
                                   Performing Arts at Middlesex University,
                                   United Kingdom

Graham RAWLINSON   is Director of Enterprise in Higher Education
                                   at the University of Surrey, United Kingdom

Stephen REEVE   is Senior Lecturer in Economics in the
                                   Department of Business Management at the
                                   University of Brighton

Professor John STEPHENSON   is Project Director, Higher Education for
                                   Capability based in Leeds Metropolitan
                                   University and the University of Leeds

Don TINKLER   is an Educational Consultant based in
                                   Victoria, Australia

PRINCIPAL ABBREVIATIONS
USED IN THE TEXT

CNAA	Council for National Academic Awards
CQSW	Certificate for Qualification in Social Work
DIP HE	Diploma of Higher Education
DTAG	Development Training Advisory Group
EHE	Enterprise in Higher Education
HEFC	Higher Education for Capability (till 1991; HEC thereafter)
HMI	Her Majesty's Inspectorate
LEA	Local Education Authority
LML	Learner-managed-learning
NFER	National Foundation for Educational Research
NGT	Nominal Group Technique
OU	Open University
PBL	Problem-based learning
PEL	Polytechnic of East London (till 1992; thereafter, University of East London)
RSA	Royal Society for the Encouragement of Arts, Manufactures and Commerce
SIP	Situation Improvement Package
SIS(a)	School for Independent Study, Polytechnic of East London
SIS(b)	Situation Improvement Summary
TVEI	Training and Vocational Education Initiative
UEL	University of East London
UWSM	University of Western Sydney, Macarthur
WEF	World Education Fellowship
YMCA	Young Men's Christian Association
YTS	Youth Training Scheme

PREFACE

In 1990, three very different bodies concerned with education came together to organise an international conference on Learner-Managed-Learning. The *World Education Fellowship (WEF)* was established in 1921 as a voluntary association concerned with learner-centred education at all levels, from pre-school through to adult and continuing education. The WEF has sections in over 20 countries and is recognised as having Consultative status to UNESCO as a Non-Government Organisation. The WEF has played a prominent role in the progressive education movement in the Twentieth Century, and has included Dewey, Piaget, Jung and Beatrice Ensor amongst its supporters.

The Royal Society for the encouragement of Arts, Manufactures and Commerce (RSA) was established in London in 1754. In 1980 it launched *Education for Capability*, a national campaign backed by educationists, business, politicians and members of the community to campaign for education - for all ages - to be more responsive and relevant to the world outside. The aim was to help all learners to become more able to cope with the demands of living and working in increasingly complex and changing circumstances at work and in the community.

North East London Polytechnic (later to become the University of East London) was a typical public sector institution of higher education offering courses at diploma and degree levels in a range of subject areas. In 1974 it set up a *School for Independent Study* (SIS) to provide a different kind of learning experience aimed at helping students to plan and complete their own programmes of study leading to Diplomas of Higher Education and Honours Degrees.

Each of these organisations promotes learner-managed-learning as the principal means of achieving its educational aims. Education for Capability argues that students will develop confidence in their ability to cope with a changing world if they have experience of being 'responsible and accountable for their own learning, as individuals and in association with others'. The WEF believes that if people are given 'the freedom... to experience and explore according to their potentialities, they will be totally involved with life itself, and grow fully to contribute their best to society as well as to their own happiness'. The School for Independent Study believes that the experience of successfully coping with their own education helps people to believe in their own power to perform, in whatever walk of life they choose. All three see the value of learner-managed-learning both in terms of personal fulfilment and effective participation in the community.

Learner-managed-learning presents many challenges for teachers and administrators. The conference in London in 1990 brought together 400 people drawn from each organisation to share their experiences. Some of that experience and that of a follow on conference in Czechoslovakia, is presented in this book and we hope readers will find something within its chapters which relates to their own experiences of education, either as a consumer or a provider.

John Stephenson, Chairman World Education Fellowship, Director Higher Education for Capability.

CHAPTER 1

INTRODUCTION

By

Norman Graves

Preamble

This book results from two conferences held in April 1990 in London and in September 1991 in Opava, Czechoslovakia.These conferences were jointly sponsored by the Polytechnic of East London (PEL),now the University of East London(U of E L), the Royal Society of Arts (RSA) and the World Education Fellowship (WEF), each of these bodies having an interest in promoting a form of non-traditional education which can be encompassed by the concept of Learner-Managed-Learning(LML). In the case of PEL the interest arose from its experience in developing courses of `Independent Study' for adults who could not or would not fit into traditional higher education courses. The RSA was then involved in promoting ` Education For Capability' in both secondary and higher education, whilst the WEF is an international organization which had pioneered `progressive education' at all levels.

The first conference having been an outstanding success, the organizers felt that given the political and other changes then going on in Eastern Europe, it was appropriate to run a similar conference in one of the former Communist States. Subsequently the Guiding Committee of the WEF felt that some of the contributions to both conferences should be preserved in book form and undertook to publish these.

Whilst the ideas and practices of LML apply right across the spectrum of education, both conferences produced more papers that were concerned with Further and Higher Education than with the Primary and Secondary stages. Consequently an editorial decision was taken to focus in this book on Further and Higher Education in order to limit its coverage and to prevent it from being too long. Nevertheless some references are made to school education and one chapter is mainly concerned with exploring the theoretical underpinnings of learner-managed-learning at the school stage(Chapter 15), whilst another(Chapter 13) looks at the necessary conditions for the introduction of learner-managed-learning into schools.

Brief historical review

Whilst the term Learner-Managed-Learning(LML) is of relatively recent vintage, the concept behind it is not. In essence it is a concept that encompasses a whole family of ideas about learners being actively engaged in the process of their own education. The socratic dialogue was an attempt at making the student think about what s/he was supposed to be learning, rather than getting him\her to memorize information. Whilst medieval theological disputations may have had some of the trappings of dialogue, they lacked the open-endedness of LML since the objectives were to arrive at conclusions that fitted the current religious dogma. With the Renaissance came a more tolerant view of knowledge acquisition and, as Professor Burgess points out in Chapter 13, Komensky is often thought of as the educator who first publicly advocated active as against passive learning in his Great Didactic of 1657. These ideas were further developed by Rousseau in the the 18th century, by Pestalozzi, Herbart and Froebel in the 19th century and by Dewey and many others in the 20th century(Entwistle,1970). However, all these pioneers of active learning were more concerned with school education or the education of infants than with adult education.

It is perhaps as well to remind ourselves that formal education for all children is a relatively recent phenomenon in the western world and that education and training for most adults is still a matter being hotly debated. But while in schools it had generally been accepted in the second half of the 20th century that no education worth its name could take place without the active involvement of the pupil, hence for example, the emphasis on enquiry learning, in adult education, the attention given to teaching methods and styles of learning has until recently been very limited. To some extent the reason for the neglect androgogy(in contradistinction to pedagogy) can be traced to the voluntary nature of much adult education; the students were already motivated to follow certain courses, they did not need motivating in the way many children do.Further most teachers in adult education had had no formal training in the skills of teaching, neither had they followed any courses in education theory. Many were part-time teachers taking time off from their normal professional activities to give adult learners the benefits of their knowledge, skills and experience.

With the growth of Further and Higher Education, and the consequent widening of the intake, problems of teaching,learning and of curriculum became more evident(Graves, 1988).

Learner-Managed-Learning

Learner-Managed-Learning is not a simple method of ensuring that students learn what they are supposed to learn. Rather does it stand for a whole range of attitudes, teaching strategies, curriculum schemes and course designs which place the student at the focal point of the learning activities to ensure his/her involvement throughout the process.The student is involved in deciding what to learn, how to learn and how that learning will be assessed (see the analysis by Len Cairns in Chapter 11). Belief in the liberating effects of LML is expressed briefly by Eunice Hinds in a final chapter. It should not be thought, however, that learner-managed-learning is a panacea for all educational ills. The various authors of chapters in this book indicate clearly that there are problems with this approach; problems which relate to student and teacher acceptance (Chapters 7 and 14), problems of pupil guidance (Chapter 16), and problems of assessment (Chapters 9 and 10). No educational technique or system is independent of the personnel operating it, thus the quality of the teacher is still paramount.

Section A of this book illustrates the practice of LML in a variety of contexts: from independent study in British polytechnics/universities, to teaching health professionals in Australian universities; from the role of industrial and commercial

SECTION A:
THE PRACTICE OF
LEARNER-MANAGED-LEARNING

experience to the problem of assessing LML in Higher Education.

Section B is concerned with some of the theoretical issues raised by the practice of LML and their practical implications.What exactly is the role of the teacher in LML? How do students themselves perceive a process which is supposedly for their ultimate benefit? Does LML result in conflicting demands being made on all concerned?

Section C deals with certain policy issues which inevitably arise from the adoption of LML in institutions.How far, for example, could LML be extended not just to selected areas of Higher Education, but throughout the system? These and other issues will be debated in the pages which follow.

REFERENCES

Entwistle H (1970) Child-centred education Methuen, London

Graves N (1988) The education crisis: which way now? Christopher Helm, Bromley

THE STUDENT EXPERIENCE OF INDEPENDENT STUDY: REACHING THE PARTS OTHER PROGRAMMES APPEAR TO MISS

By

John Stephenson

'There is an awful truthfulness about independent study.
It is about yourself and there is no getting away from it'.
(Former Dip HE student)

Introduction

In 1974, the North East London Polytechnic (now known as the University of East london) gained CNAA approval for a course proposal which had no specified content, no prescribed reading lists, no timetables and no formal examinations. The course proposal consisted of a rationale, a set of procedures and criteria for validating programmes of study prepared by students themselves, and arrangements for the provision of specialist supervision and basic skill support. Students had to plan and negotiate approval for their own programmes leading to the new award of Diploma of Higher Education, thus turning traditional practice of course design and control on its head.

Such a proposal would not be so unusual today but in 1974 it was truly radical. It is a measure of the contribution of the work of the University to wider educational debate that similar proposals are being actively encouraged both in Britain and overseas. Indeed, through its Enterprise Initiative, the Government itself is sponsoring such changes in other institutions. Credit is due to those who had the vision and the courage to initiate and support the 1974 proposal, especially Professor Tyrrell Burgess, Sir Toby Weaver, and the Polytechnic's Director at that time, Dr George Brosan. Tribute must also be made to the many scores of tutors, from all parts of the Polytechnic, who have helped it flourish over the years.

In 1984, 10 years and over 1000 students later, it seemed appropriate to ask questions about the effects the experience of independent study had had on the students themselves. The Polytechnic gave me leave of absence to track down some former students, and British Petroleum plc provided some financial support. I invited a random selection of Diplomates who were at least two years out of the Polytechnic to evaluate, with the wisdom of hindsight, their experience of independent study in the context of their life histories to date.

I will concentrate on two aspects of independent study which the experience of students illuminates. The first concerns STUDENT MOTIVATION, and the second concerns the development of CAPABILITY. I will then share with you some speculations about possible implications for higher education as a whole.

Student motivation

People who meet with independent study students invariably remark on their high level of motivation and their strong personal identification with their studies. Examination of their explanations of the reasons why they applied, why they persevered and how they have benefited reveals a range of motivating factors mainly characterised by the personal benefit they most desired from their higher education. Pursuit of these personal benefits is all embracing, impinging on all aspects of students' interactions with their programmes and the polytechnic. They have the status of being the students' primary needs.

In all I distinguished **six primary needs**:

RESPECT

IDENTITY

VALUE

COMMITMENT

QUALIFICATION

TRANSFORMATION

These different needs are first identifiable in students' reasons for applying. Need for **respect** is illustrated by those who feel that their educational qualifications, jobs or personal circumstances do not accurately present their true potential and ability to the outside world. Phil told me that he was tired of people explaining long words to him just because he was a window-cleaner. He could feel people saying `Christ, let's throw clods of earth at him' whenever they saw him with his ladder. Meryl felt patronised by the professionally qualified people for whom she worked as a secretary. Both Phil and Meryl needed the respect they felt would come from participation in higher education and having recognised educational achievement. Any higher education course would do.

Typical of those with a need for **identity** was Tim who had spent many years doing a range of jobs but could not see how he related to any one of them. Jean did not dare to reveal or trust her real interest in poetry, and Brian wanted a chance to look around for something to which he could commit himself. They wanted the chance to `sort themselves out'.

The need for **value** is felt by students who have built up some expertise largely by their own efforts. They need time to `take stock' or `make sense' of their experience, and to have it recognised. Bob felt that people saying `Oh, he's self taught' did not adequately recognise his artistic ability, and Delia was looking for `some theory, to have a central focus' on her experiences as a community worker.

The need for **commitment** is felt by those who know the future they want for themselves and they want the opportunity to make it happen, to absorb themselves in their new direction. Gary turned down a scholarship to Oxford because he could not see its relevance. The Diploma in Higher Education(DIP HE) would help him become what he wanted to become.

Qualifications are to some extent relevant to all groups, but for some, the need for a qualification dominates all other considerations. Paul applied because it was the only way he could get a qualification in computing. The School of Independent Study provided him with a back-door entrance. He had been turned down for an Higher National Diploma because he had no qualifications; he is now head of the computer department in a City of London merchant bank.

The need for **transformation** involves all aspects of students' lives. These student feel they are severely constrained by circumstances and are looking to raise the level of their whole quality of life, including their careers. Julie, at the age of 18, felt totally dominated by her parents; Doreen was constantly put down by her boy-friend and employers. Each needed to break out.

Those with needs for respect or qualification would have preferred a conventional course. At that time, one was not available. This was also true to some extent for those looking for transformation.

I would suggest that these highly personal needs can be found amongst any group of students. The proposition I wish to put to you is that independent study makes two things possible. It makes it possible for students to acknowledge the importance of such personal needs, and more importantly, it enables students themselves to take actions which ensure those needs can be met through their programmes of study.

With the absence of predetermined content, independent study students find themselves, in many cases reluctantly as we shall see, in the position of having to argue for and justify what they want to do, and to do so on the basis of their own distinctive experience and longer term ambitions. This aspect of the planning of independent study programmes puts students in touch with a life-change perspective to their education, and requires them to take an active, rather than a passive role in the satisfaction of their needs as part of that life-change process. As a consequence, it is possible to characterise students' experiences by the actions they take in meeting their needs.

Students may be said to belong to the following categories:

EARNERS OF RESPECT

SEARCHERS OF IDENTITY

PROVERS OF VALUE

BUILDERS OF COMMITMENT

TAKERS OF QUALIFICATIONS

TRANSFORMERS

Independent study students are not able to be passive receivers. For instance, commitment has to be built, not received. Identity has to be searched for, not received. Respect has to be earned, not received. Value has to be proved, not received. Qualifications are taken, not received. Transformation has to be initiated and carried out, not received. The underlined words characterise the nature of different student interactions with their programmes and the Polytechnic. Independent study students are not just students; they are builders, provers, earners, takers, searchers or transformers.

The importance of these different motivations is seen when comparing the experiences of different students. Compare these reactions to the experience of planning their own programmes and receiving external validation of their proposas:-

First, the **builders** of commitment: Gary found it `quite exciting' to be `responsible for getting it together', and validation of his proposed programme made him feel `educationally supported' in what he wanted to do and made him feel `enormously privileged'. He was building his own future and the system was helping him do it.

In stark contrast, the **takers** found the business of planning to be `a chore', and an unnecessary `waste of time'. This was Moira's view: `I just wanted to get on with it but we had to play the system. I was putting things down just to get the Statement (contract) through.' When her programme was validated, Moira rejoiced because `it meant the headache had stopped' and she could at last get on with her work.

Having to plan their own courses put great pressure on the **searchers** of identity. They wanted to commit themselves to something but did not know to what. This was Brian's experience:

> `It helped me clarify the path that my life had taken to that
> present point.... it was a kind of catharsis, getting it out of my
> system... The process of validation was saying something
> about me, in that I'd clarified what it was that I wanted to do,
> and that felt pretty good. It was almost like a liberating
> experience'.

And yet a further contrast can be seen with the **earners** of respect. They needed to be seen to be succeeding in higher education so they planned courses according to the subjects most likely to lead to their success. `Find a reasonable tutor, one who was available and who told you what to do', seemed to be their major concern at that time. Validation of their proposals was important because it meant they had passed a Part One and were still on the course. Validation of their proposal also meant that they were being taken seriously.

Similar variations can be seen in the way students interact with their tutors, judge their own progress and prepare for their assessments once their validated programmes are under way. I can give only the briefest flavour.

The Takers, for instance, liked it best when their tutors gave them assignments and feedback directly relevant to getting their qualification. They leave as soon as they have the qualification that will take them forward.

Earners of respect liked getting good grades for their assignments, being involved in discussion and, above all, being taken seriously by tutors and other students. Because the Diploma in Higher Education is not recognised amongst their acquaintances, they invariably proceed to higher and more familiar qualifications such as the Honours Degree by Independent Study. If that is not recognised, they proceed to a Masters Degree. Only when they feel fully respected for their ability and worth do they begin to look for something to which they can commit themselves.

Searchers of Identity are very wary of getting too engrossed into a programme until they have tested it out as being what they really want. Formal assignments and grades do not help the searchers as much as successfully putting a possible identity to the test. Once an identity is found, progress is dramatic. Let me quote from Jean, the closet poet, describing the most significant moment of her whole independent study experience:

> `I put forward the proposal that I wanted to do my own poetry and he (my tutor) was very nasty and he said "give me your poetry" and that was the first time ever that I had handed it over to someone who wasn't sympathetic. It was one of the biggest risks I had ever taken.*
>
> *I knew he had it in him to turn round and say "This is crap". He didn't. He said "Thank goodness, you CAN write poetry."`*

With this confirmation, Jean progressed very rapidly, and gained a Degree in her own poetry. She is now publishing her work and is using poetry-writing as an aid to the dying.

Builders judge their own progress in the field for which they are preparing themselves. Tutors are useful in helping them talk things through. Gary, for instance, became impatient with having to complete his programme once he realised that he had acquired the skills he needed in order to practice his new vocation.

The significance of all this is threefold:

First, students with very different needs are able to use independent study for their own purposes, and to get what they want out of it. Flexibility relates to student need as much as to content.

Second, student motivation is strong because students are able to relate their studies, and how they pursue them, to their own personal needs;

Third, awareness of the characteristics of different primary needs can help tutors and students get the most out of their interactions. The kind of feedback most useful for a taker of qualifications, for instance, would not be too helpful to a searcher of identity.

The internal dimension

What sense can be made of these different kinds of experience? What light do they shed on the underlying processes of independent study?

At first sight, it might appear that the differences between students can be characterised as being `intrinsic' or `extrinsic'. To some extent that is right but only up to a point. There are two different aspects:

the focus of reference and

the focus of development,

each of which has an internal and an external dimension, as illustrated in the diagram below

In Figure 2.1, the *focus of development* refers to the general purpose of the student. An *internal focus of development,* for instance, refers to a concern about changing the self. An *external focus of development* refers to a concern to develop skills and knowledge for some outward context or application.

Fig 2.1. STUDENTS' PRIMARY FOCUS GRID.

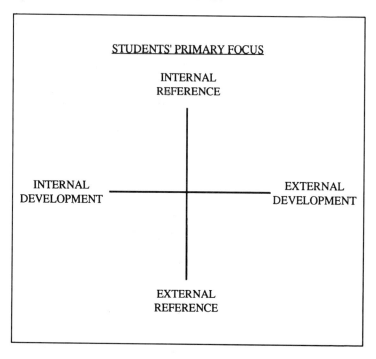

The *focus of reference* refers to a student's general inclination towards self-direction or towards the direction or opinions of others.

When they are presented in a grid-form, there are four basic general student orientations. It is possible to place each of the student styles within the grid as follows (Fig 2.2):

Figure 2.2 shows, for instance, that whilst both commitment and qualification are about the external application of skills and knowledge, the essential difference between them is that commitment involves much more of an internal focus of reference than does a concern for qualifications alone.

Similarly, the concern for identity and the concern for respect are both about the internal development of the student. The qualitative differences between the experiences of the searcher for identity and the earner of respect are accounted for by their different focus of reference.

Concern for proving the value of your own experience involves both an external and an internal focus of development because the students concerned are seeking external recognition for expertise which they themselves have developed and wish to take forward. The Transformers move rapidly from section to section.

The qualification sector is the only sector without any internal dimension, either of reference or of development. The takers of qualifications were the students who most wanted to join a conventional course, if only they could find a conventional course to take them.

The intriguing question is whether conventional courses are able to meet needs other than the need for qualification. Do people who are strongly internally referenced, for instance, keep away from conventional qualification-focused education? Do they suppress their preference for self-direction or use it within the non-curriculum activities like the students union? Do conventional courses in effect persuade people that education is not about internal-referenced concerns such as respect, identity, commitment, value and personal transformation?

Fig 2.2 MOTIVATIONAL TYPES ACCORDING TO STUDENTS' PRIMARY FOCUS

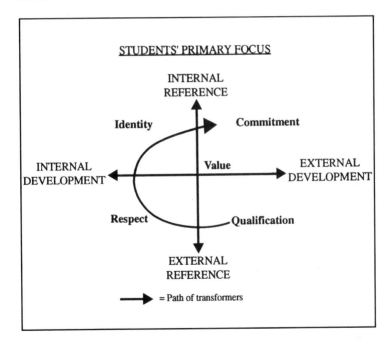

I have found the student focus grid - without the descriptive labels of respect, identity etc - to be a very useful tool to help students explore their own motivation. Post-graduate students in another institution were able to plot their own general disposition, and very few placed themselves in the external / external quarter.

It would be an interesting exercise to see how students generally in the university might rate themselves. I suspect that the independent study students are not eccentric. There are many who, like them, are internally referenced but who have learned to associate education with external reference behaviour. They must either endure it or not bother at all.

There is one further important observation to make about the internal /external dimension. As the students moved through their programmes, whether internally or externally referenced, they had no option but to take responsibility for some of their work, particularly the preparation of material for their own assessment. Students who were already internally referenced became more confident in themselves; those who were externally referenced discovered they could also be internally referenced. The Transformers are the most dramatic examples of this tendency but it applies to most of the students in my sample. The course requirement that students should take responsibility gives students real experience of taking responsibility. There is a net movement towards the internally referenced.

The drift to an internal focus of reference through their independent study programme can be seen in the experiences of those former independent study students who moved on to conventionally taught courses.

Fiona (a builder of commitment), for instance, said of her teachers' certificate course that students `weren't allowed any self-expression or control'; she enlisted the help of a neighbouring university in organising a questionnaire to help her course to cater `for the needs of the students'. Delia, a prover, found her university post-graduate diploma programme in psychology `atrocious'; she could learn it better herself. Doreen, a transformer, found her post-graduate professional conversion course `frustrating... a straight jacket... work that I had already done to a greater depth. I arranged my own alternative'. Jim, a transformer, describes his experiences on a Certificate for Qualification in Social Work(CQSW) course as follows:

> *It was a very structured course. I told them "There's no way*
> *I'm going to stick through lectures" and (the tutor) said "If*
> *you are prepared to take the risk, what we will do is we will*
> *give you an extension from lectures for a whole term. If at the*
> *end of that term all your essay marks are O.K., you do it in*
> *any way you want". I got A's and B's in all of them.*

More interestingly and significantly is the experience of those who were originally strongly externally referenced on joining the Diploma course. Moira, as a taker, was one of those who said on entry onto the Dip H E programme `I would have preferred a set course'. She was pleased to have transferred to `a normal course at last' for her post-Dip HE education. The culture of student control which she had resisted on her Dip HE programme had obviously rubbed off on her because she soon discovered that `lectures ...(were) not the most efficient use of our time' and that she `would have chosen a more varied reading list' than the one given to her by her tutors. She then realised that it was a matter of her `extracting the value of what I am doing, for my needs, and what I need to learn'. She got a first class honours degree. Sally, another originally external referenced student, found that her fellow MA students in a major university, faced with establishing the independence necessary for the production of a dissertation, were `sort of worried because they wanted help.... I knew what I had to do and just got on with it... I know it's because of the independent study.'

A further indication of the development of internal reference comes from comparing students' current self-perceptions with their self-perceptions prior to applying to the Dip HE. The following grid (Fig 2.3) shows how they feel their level of independence and their commitment to what they are doing has changed as a result of their independent study.

Fig 2.3 <u>STUDENT SELF PERCEPTIONS</u>
<u>PRE - DIP HE AND NOW</u>

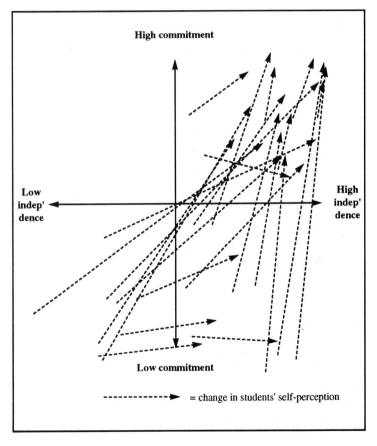

In the Student Self-Perceptions grid, (Fig. 2.3.) every one of the first 24 students interviewed reported feeling more independent as a result of their independent study. Some of them, mainly the transformers, reported a dramatic increase in both independence and commitment. Others, mainly the earners of respect, reported increases in independence but little growth in commitment.

One student actually experienced a decrease in her commitment to artwork as a direct result of her independent study. Her tutor ignored her need to build her own commitment and imposed on her a programme designed to get her a qualification. Pushing her from an internal reference into the mould of the external reference reduced her commitment. Overall, the changes in student self-perception indicated in Figure 2.3. suggest that giving externally referenced students direct experience of internal reference increases their independence and, in many cases, also increases their commitment.

The development of independent capability

I would have liked to tell you what all the students in the sample are currently doing with their lives. However, I will briefly describe a few who illustrate a general feature observable in most.

Kenny is a Director of a City company specialising in headhunting for accountants. His course was in underwater technology. He puts his success down to his insight that his job is not about accounting. It is about understanding the needs of individual people and organisations and being able to bring them together. Delia runs a refuge and rescue service for alcoholics. She has to secure funds, premises, support from unsympathetic councils; she has to train staff. She uses an adaptation of the Dip HE planning activity as an effective means of getting clients to `get a grip of themselves'. Denny was denied entry to Business studies courses so he designed his own. He now runs 4 separate businesses and is planning a major new investment. The Dip HE gave him the `nerve' to give it a go. There are successful teachers and community workers, most of whom have or are securing promotion or positions of responsibility. One has recently made himself unemployed, and the one whose experiences in art were unsatisfactory describes herself as working as a housewife. All the others are in paid or fee-earning activity.

A dominant characteristic of former independent study students, hinted at in these brief cameos, is their strong belief in their own power to perform. Confidence in the power to take effective action seems to have the status of a general outcome of independent study as shown by this selection of student comments about their overall gain from their experience:-

> *I don't think that anything is beyond me.*
>
> *I have the confidence to do almost anything, to try almost anything.*
>
> *I can cope with most things that people can throw at me now.*
>
> *It's like finding a muscle you haven't used.*
>
> *I know I can do it whatever it is... I think my personal power is now much higher.*
>
> *I feel autonomous, much more confident in my own ability.*
>
> *My level of confidence is based on fact, not myth... am much*

more in control.

I've got the confidence to actually do it as well.

I know now that when I make decisions I will actually carry them through and that I CAN carry them through.

I now know that I can really do it.

Confidence to do almost anything, to try almost anything.

A feeling of being able to get up and do something.

You can do what you want to do and not follow the sheep.

I know I can do it now.

I previously would not have had the nerve to do what I am doing.

Each of above statements was made by a different person. They are only a selection. They represent students' own reflections on the overall value of their independent study experience. Closer analysis of students' fuller explanations of their confidence in their 'power to perform' reveals three separate and inter-related components (Fig 2.4).

(see OHP file)

Fig 2.4   THREE COMPONENTS OF PERSONAL POWER TO PERFORM
COMPONENTS OF CAPABILITY

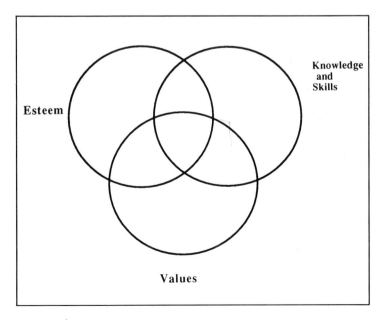

Esteem

Knowledge
and
Skills

Values

First, they have confidence in themselves as people; they have greatly enhanced **self-esteem** as illustrated by these statements by different students:

> *It has given me a lot more confidence to talk to people at different levels.*
>
> *I'm more self-assured and confident.*
>
> *I feel more able to instigate things... with people in authority.*
>
> *Independent Study gives you a certain feeling of self-worth.*
>
> *I'm a lot more secure in myself... I have a higher opinion of myself.*
>
> *It gives students formal acknowledgement of where they are.*
>
> *I can now say no.*
>
> *I can now look other people in the eye.. I feel much better about myself.*
>
> *(Independent study is) a means of helping people to value themselves.*
>
> *I have the ability to criticise myself.*
>
> *I do not feel threatened if I don't know something.*
>
> *(I am) no longer feeling embarrassed about everything I did... definitely self-esteem has come out of it.*

Second, the students have confidence in their **judgments and values**: i.e they have confidence in their ability to make judgments, have opinions and to be decisive. Some more extracts from a range of students illustrate the point:-

> *I certainly express my opinions more freely.*
>
> *I have a lot more confidence in my own ability and judgment.*
>
> *It has allowed me to make my own decisions.*
>
> *I am much clearer in what I want and what I don't want.*
>
> *I am more ready to take a decision.*
>
> *It built up my confidence in... trusting my judgment about things.*
>
> *I am quite prepared to argue whereas before I would get all timid.*
>
> *I'm now much more confident to back my judgment and take things on.*
>
> *As a person you feel you're independent, you're a free agent, you can decide for yourself.*
>
> *I've learned how to cope with dilemmas.*
>
> *I've got an opinion about world affairs.*
>
> *Now I question a lot.*
>
> *I have the ability to criticise myself - and I decide things for myself.*

The third component of their personal power is confidence in the soundness and relevance of their **skills and knowledge**, and in their **ability to acquire new skills and knowledge when appropriate**. Here is a selection of the many statements students have made about their confidence in their ability to continue to learn through their own initiative:-

> *It gave me the skills to acquire the information that I need at any given time for anything.*
>
> *If I don't know something I know I can find it out.*
>
> *(I can) decide priorities of what to learn and to pick out information.*
>
> *Anything I want to know now I can teach myself.*
>
> *I am more confident about finding things out for myself.*
>
> *I enjoyed studying - I don't ever want to stop.*
>
> *I enjoy working with others because that is one of the ways in which I learn.*

All of these statements about esteem, values, and skills and knowledge have a distinct internal flavour about them. Collectively, they describe students who have an **independent capability**. They therefore chime with the earlier proposition that independent study promotes students' internal focus of reference. It seems appropriate, therefore, to speculate what these three components might look like if they had an external focus of reference. Or, to put it another way, how does **independent capability** differ from **dependent capability**.

Table 2.1 is one attempt to define the difference:-

Table 2.1

INDEButtonEND AND DEPENDENT CAPABILITY

	DEPENDENT CAPABILITY	INDEPENDENT CAPABILITY
Knowledge and Skills	Received	Learned
	Tested by others	Self-monitored
	Relevance determined by others	Relevance negotiated by self
	Fragmented	Integrated adaptable and extendable
	Prescribed application	
Esteem	Labels, status uniforms	Proved self-worth
	Recognized qualification	Confidence in own ability
	Failure = threat	Failure = opportunity
		Trusts intuition
Value	Priorities set by others	Can set own priorities
	Avoids judgements	Trust in own judgement

Though they may be highly skilled and knowledgeable, the **dependently capable** are likely to have acquired their expertise through instruction, training and supervised practice, mastering known procedures or solutions which deal with predictable situations or problems. In totally new situations, where the context is unfamiliar or when entirely new problems appear, they will need retraining or strong guidance. They derive their esteem from their formal status, their certificated expertise and the authority of those they represent. They aim to eliminate error by using tried and tested techniques; any failure is seen as a threat to their expertise. When unfamiliar situations or problems arise and judgments are needed the dependently capable will seek guidance from superiors and will expect priorities to be set by those in authority.

At the other extreme, the **independently capable** are confident in their expertise and in their understanding of its internal interconnectedness. It has been learned, not given. Having been responsible for its acquisition, they know they can adapt or extend it when necessary. They have confidence in their own worth, both as individuals and as experts in their own right. With an inner confidence in themselves, one which is not dependent upon how others perceive them, they see error or failure as opportunity for learning, not as a threat. They trust their intuition. When faced with unfamiliar situations, they are prepared to back their own judgments, even to take risks, in order to explore new ideas. They know they can learn from the experience.

The importance of being able to distinguish between dependent and independent capability can be shown as follows (Fig 2.5) :

The capability required for Position Y in Figure 2.5. is one which is able to service the needs of familiar situations, with predictable problems with well-known information. Such situations may even require a high degree of skill and considerable specialist knowledge but once such skills and knowledge have been acquired their application is relatively straightforward.

As one moves away from the predictability ends of the problem / context axes there is a greater need for a more flexible and responsive capability, where one is able to make judgments, acquire new skills and knowledge, use the skills of others and take calculated risks. There is a greater need for confidence in one's personal power to perform. The closer one is to Position Z, the greater the need for an independent capability.

The evidence from the students who completed their higher education by independent study suggests that their confidence in their own power to perform - that is, in their independent capability - derives directly from their experience of taking responsibility for their own development, for their own life-change, for the satisfaction of deeply relevant personal needs and for the acquisition of relevant skills and knowledge, by their own efforts. They achieved all of these within the unfamiliar and demanding context of higher education. In short, they proved they could take it on.

Explanation of the relevance of independent study to the development of their confidence in their power to perform comes from the students' themselves:-

> *It's the fact that you know that you did it.*
>
> *I think the fact that you are actually required to input so much and rely on your own resources so much actually gives you much greater confidence about independence and ability to actually fend for yourself.*
>
> *It works because you have to cope with it.*

Fig 2.5   <u>DEPENDENT AND INDEPENDENT CAPABILITY</u>

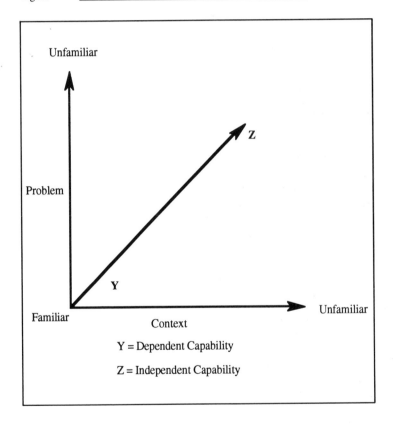

Evidence of how independent study helps with learning is shown by the freedom students feel for the making and learning from mistakes, and the experience it gives of being responsible for their own learning:

> *It gave a great space to make mistakes again, to rebuild a confidence.*

The opportunity to fail - that's where learning takes place.. it is acceptable to learn from mistakes.

(What makes it work?) - the person taking responsibility for their own learning - it places much more importance on learning than teaching. It was the first formalised kind of programme I had done where it was really valid to learn in that way.

You have to get off your backside and go and find out and it wasn't that difficult.. you learn from it.. you don't get supervision, you get help.

These comments on learning from mistakes present an interesting challenge. Being at ease with risking getting something wrong on the grounds that such experience is the basis of learning, is an essential feature of survival in position Z. It would be interesting to discover the extent to which conventional higher education programmes actually deny students opportunities to learn from mistakes. How many courses present their students with tightly defined content, prescriptive reading lists, carefully planned notes and lectures directly focused on the questions known to be in the examination paper? How many work on the proposition that students must be protected at all cost from the risk of failure, and must be nurtured every step of the way? Is there more concern for lecturers' 'pass-rates', than for the education of students?

At this point I wish to make an important aside. The kind of experiences I have been describing are not the experiences of therapy, as some critics have suggested. They are experiences of personal development through education, tested within what is normally seen to be the business of higher education, namely the pursuit of excellence. None of the needs I have described can be met to the satisfaction of the students themselves without rigorous scrutiny of their own achievements. Respect is best earned, for instance, when the students themselves know they have achieved at least the levels achieved by other graduates, not at some compensatory level. Value, identity and commitment are best tested against the rigours of the field itself, the reactions of clients, the recognition of acknowledged experts, or even the publication of their work. Qualifications have to be tradable on the open market. The most productive environment for independent study is one which combines mutual support with rigour and high aspiration.

Some implications for higher education

I would like to make a few observations about the wider relevance of this experience to higher education as a whole.

Any society in which progress and change are common features requires its people to be independently capable . It should be a distinctive role of higher education, as opposed to intensive training, to prepare people with real capacity for managing and coping with change and uncertainty. The speed of technological, economic and social change means our jobs and circumstances change more frequently and less predictably than before. The explosion in the expansion of specialist knowledge (doubling every 8 years by one estimate), puts a premium on giving people confidence in their own ability to learn and shows how futile it is to try to sustain the formal transmission of knowledge model of higher education. Major employers now recognise the importance of these personal qualities of independent capability in their graduate recruitment. They also know they do not find them in the normal round of graduate recruitment. One of the world's largest business companies no longer seeks to recruit graduates of business studies programmes to its higher positions because they find them lacking in flexibility, openness and the ability to continue learning for themselves.

At a series of seminars for chairs of leading companies, Vice-Chancellors and Polytechnic Directors held at the Royal Society for the encouragement of Arts, Manufactures and Commerce (RSA), the overwhelming consensus was that the time was now right for higher education to find more ways of helping more students to develop the qualities of independent capability.

Agreeing that graduates should be independently capable is one thing. Knowing how to help them develop such qualities is another. Many institutions are attempting to meet the need by `bolt-on' activities on the assumption that the skills and qualities of personal capability can be achieved as extras, and through traditional teacher - student relationships. Students, it is argued by advocates of this approach, can be helped to cope with problems by being given problems to cope with - as exercises. Students can be helped to learn how to learn by being given instruction in learning methods. Values clarification can be pursued within the context of teacher-organised seminars.

The problem with this teacher-led approach is that it assumes that possession of skills is in itself enough. It misses entirely the point about the development of people's confidence in their power to perform their skills in different situations. Only when the full importance of the need to foster students' internally focused power to perform is it appreciated that students need to have real experience of exercising such power as part of their course. Moreover, there is much educational research elsewhere which suggests that directly involving students in their mainstream courses, actually enhances their level of understanding of key concepts and raises the general quality of their work.

When one adds the opportunity independent study gives for students to address their own deep personal needs, to develop their personal independence and commitment, and to acquire publicly recognised qualifications, what emerges is an impressive amount of `value added'. Furthermore, 9 out of 10 of the students lacked normal entry requirements, and they represented a very wide variety of personal circumstances.

The sum effect of the experience of independent study reported to me by former students, lends support for an otherwise fading slogan, not normally applied to education: `the medium is the message'. Confidence in one's capability is developed through having to be capable on one's course.

I have not sought to comment on the adequacy of the procedures and practices of the existing independent study programmes. I am not the most appropriate person to do so. The student experiences on which I have reported do have one clear implication for the increasing numbers of teachers who wish to help students to develop their specialist expertise, their personal potential and their capability. It is simply this: find as many different ways as you can for giving more students more opportunities to have more responsibility for their own learning.

The Polytechnic of East London was, in this respect at least, a national and international leader. It has long since learned how to cope with learner responsibility within the academic, political and financial constraints of a large and complex public institution. It is easier to see the enormity of this collective achievement from outside the institution than it is from within. The Polytechnic (now University) has sufficient experience from which many new applications can be devised within the context of existing specialist programmes.

Many institutions in this country and overseas are finding new ways, both small and large scale, of giving students more responsibility for their own learning. I hope these will not be limited within the confines of an independent study programmes.

REFERENCE

Taylor, M (1986), Learning for Self-Direction in the Classroom: The Pattern of a Transition Process, <u>Journal of Studies in Higher Education</u>, 11 (1), pp 55-72.

CHAPTER 3

ENTERPRISE IN HIGHER EDUCATION AND LEARNER-MANAGED-LEARNING: THE USE OF LEARNING CONTRACTS

By

MIKE LAYCOCK

Introduction

The Enterprise in Higher Education initiative was announced by HM Government in December 1987 and implementation in specific institutions began in October 1988. The initiative is intended to develop higher education, through mutually agreed and contracted processes of curriculum change, so as to produce more enterprising students. Contracts of up to £1 million over five years have been offered to over 40 institutions in the first three rounds of the initiative with a further 15 selected for the current fourth round.

The principal aims of the initiative are that:

1)   "every person seeking a higher education qualification should be able to develop competencies and aptitudes relevant to enterprise"; and

2)   "these competencies should be acquired at least in part through project based work, designed to be undertaken in a real economic setting, and they should be jointly assessed by employers and the higher education institutions". (Department of Employment,1991)

EHE seeks to effect curriculum change which is predominantly process rather than content related and oriented towards two specific themes of the developing scheme; the move towards active, experiential learning styles and the relevance of the curriculum to the world of work. Curriculum development is seen as a continuous and evolutionary process brought about by building on existing strengths.

Throughout the literature of the Enterprise in Higher Education initiative are references to the importance of increasing "student responsibility in learning". The latest Employment Department document publicising the "Key Features of Enterprise in Higher Education " reiterates the philosophy stating that "Traditional teaching methods are giving way to more participative and activity-based styles, where enterprising qualities are encouraged and rewarded. Students need increasingly to develop responsibility of their own lifelong learning" (Department of Employment,1991). The accent on Learner-Managed-Learning is clearly emphasised and referred to repeatedly, viz:

-       "The change in learning styles consists of a trend away from delivery of
        lectures towards greater use of project work, case studies, simulations,
        quasi businesses, discussion, computer aided learning packages and
        independent learning" (Department of Employment,1991).

-       "EHE encourages change to student-centred styles of learning. Implicit
        is the assumption that students will be active participants in the
        programme, increasingly involved in negotiating their own learning
        programmes" (Department of Employment,1991).

From pedagogy to androgogy

The shift in educational practice is clearly from a pedagogical to an androgogical
model with an alternative set of assumptions about the "enterprising" value of
specific learning styles. Enterprising learning explicitly seeks to promote a move
away from an historical legacy in which, as Knowles has argued, "our entire
educational enterprise, including higher education, was frozen in a pedagogical
model" (Knowles,1990). Knowles believes the pedagogical model permits the
teacher to take full responsibility for decisions about what is to be learned, how it is
to be learned, when it is to be learned and if it has been learned, leaving the learner
with a submissive role. The move is from teacher-centred to student-centred, from
didactic to facilitative teaching from dependent to autonomous study, from
transmission to interpretation, from the authoritarian to the democratic.

For all individual Universities involved, the practical interpretation of EHE has
increasingly shifted from course content and syllabus requirements towards the
development of student skills and qualities learned and practised both inside and
outside the institution. A recent NFER survey of institutions involved in EHE
concluded that:

        "The shift in focus implies a shift in teaching and learning strategies
        away from the traditional transmissive mode of formal lectures, towards
        an emphasis on students' responsibility for their own learning...... Thus
        the traditional emphasis on content-led, lecturer-dominated courses,
        transmitting largely theoretical or propositional knowledge and
        examined formally in end-of-course written examinations is to be shifted
        into a different conceptual framework. In this framework students
        would construct knowledge rather than receive it; would do so with
        greater independence and opportunity to work in small groups and
        would be assessed by procedures which acknowledge the nature and
        context of their learning" (NFER,1991).

The RSA Higher Education for Capability (HEFC) campaign, launched in
November 1988 similarly argues that "how a student learns in formal education is a
critical factor in the development of capability" (Royal Society of Arts,1991) and
aims to generate national debate to promote student responsibility in learning.
HEFC believes that "Individuals, industry and society will benefit from a well-
balanced education, concerned not only with the acquisition of knowledge and
skills of analysis, but also with excellence in using and communicating knowledge,
doing, making, designing, collaborating, organising and creating" (Royal Society of

Arts,1991).

The "Enterprise learning programme" at the University of East London

The Polytechnic (now University) of East London which was successful in the third round of the EHE initiative, has built its distinctive Programme on existing institutional strengths and is setting out to develop the competence, flexibility and resourcefulness of both its students and staff.

The aims of the Programme are:

- to facilitate the development of a learning process, in all courses throughout the University, which actively encourages students as individuals and as members of learning groups to take greater responsibility for their own learning; and

- to create a learning environment in which the approval and assessment of students' programmes of study are conducted in partnership between the student, the institution and employers/practitioners.

The interpretation of "student responsibility in learning" adopted by the Programme is that students, both individually and in collaboration, take an active part in planning, monitoring and organising their own learning and providing evidence of achievement against intended outcomes. The principal mechanism by which such responsibility can be exercised and managed by the learner is the Learning Contract.

The learning contract

A particular reliance is placed on the injection of Learning Contracts into the University's courses. The objective over the five years is that over 7,000 students will be using them for many aspects of their learning but particularly for placement, work experience, project work or any form of experiential learning which might involve negotiation with employer partners.

To the uninformed, the term Learning Contract might imply a legalistic, bureaucratic, mechanistic approach to learning. A "negotiated learning plan" might better express the process. The starting point for the development of the Contract is a decision about its structure. Though a model plan will necessarily reflect the context of its intended use, the following series of issues might be addressed by the student.

1   An identification of existing strengths and weaknesses in skills, knowledge and experience.

A useful starting point for all students but particularly for adult learners is the formal acknowledgement of prior learning. Such a record has elsewhere been referred to as a "Profile" or may be a previous "Record of Achievement". Depending on its presentation it may also be used by admissions tutors as a means of accrediting prior learning. For all students it is a positive signifier of progress.

2   The aims and objectives of the proposed study.

The setting of clear aims and objectives is a fundamental part of professional life and consistent practice in their determination is of obvious importance.

3   The skills development required for the study.

Specific attention can be given to the skills requirement of the particular study. Depending on its nature, the development of problem-solving skills, teamwork skills or presentation skills may be seen as integral to the fulfilment of objectives.

4   The content, context and operation of the study.

Accurately defining a complete action plan for the study may be a complex process specifying the content, wider contextual implications, the proposed methods and timescale.

5   The resource implications of the study.

Resources for the study may include both human and material resources, indicating institutional and employer supervision, access to academic learning resource material, laboratory facilities.

6   A justification of the relationship between the study, future development and intended employment.

Justifying the plan requires the student to address the credibility of what is proposed and to locate learning in terms of personal development.

7   A clear statement of products or outcomes of the study to be submitted for assessment.

Clearly the invitation to the student is to address key issues such as level of performance required to secure external accreditation in the submission, for example, of reports, essays, dissertations, software, artefacts etc.

Implications for educators

Of central concern to educators in enabling students to take responsibility for planning, monitoring and organising their learning is that of the credibility of, or public confidence in, that which is undertaken. Where academics are traditionally the guardians of quality, content, level and monitors of progress, here the challenge is to find ways of acknowledging student involvement in such activities.

Implications for employers

Where, as in the University's Programme, the Learning Contract may seek to structure learning in employer contexts, the involvement of employers in reassuring students of the relevance of their programmes and providing experiences in response to student objectives, implies continuous participation in the learning process.

Resource-based learning

A student-centred approach, rather than a discipline-, subject- or module-centred approach, also implies a shift away from directed learning to resource-based learning. Academic staff respond to the needs and interest of students by acting as a facilitative resource, providing relevant materials. Employers provide work placement and supervisory resources. Control rests with the student.

The tripartite co-operative partnership

Providing for student responsibility <u>and</u> public credibility while acting as a resource involves a staged participation by the three parties (student/institution/employer). First all parties should be involved in negotiating the Learning Contract. Second all parties should participate in the approval of the Contract. Approval can be managed with appropriate degrees of formality. When the learning involved is to be formally accredited, formal approval procedures may need to be addressed.

Once approval has been secured then students, tutors and employer partners can proceed to implementation, secure in the knowledge that successful completion can be publicly recognised. Finally, all parties should be involved in assessment both to determine the extent to which the learning, as approved, has been completed and at what level. (Fig 3.1)

Fig 3.1   <u>PARTNERSHIP IN THE LEARNING CONTRACT</u>

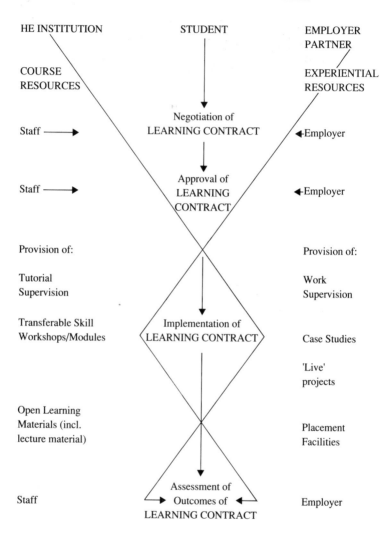

Students, educators and employers can derive benefit from such an androgogical approach to co-operative education. There is much confirmation that involving students in the design of their programmes of study represents a powerful philosophy for adult education. It increases motivation, promotes understanding of fundamentals and focuses students on the wider relevance of their studies. Mezirow, for example, argues that helping learners translate experience in such a way as they may understand their problems and the options open to them, so that they can take responsibility for their decision-making is the essence of education. His support is progressed by a "Charter for Androgogy" which can assist learners to learn in a way that enhances their capability to function as self-directed learners. Such a perspective must:

> - progressively decrease the learners dependency on the educator;

> - help the learner understand how to use learning resources;

> - assist the learner to define his/her learning needs;

> - assist learners to assume increasing responsibility for defining learning objectives, planning their own programme and assessing their progress;

> - organise what is to be learned;

> - foster learner decision making;

> - encourage the use of criteria for judging;

> - foster a self-corrective, reflexive approach to learning;

> - facilitate problem posing and problem-solving;

> - reinforce the self-concept of the learner as a learner;

> - emphasize experiential, participative and projective instructional methods;

> - make a moral distinction between helping the learner understand a range of choices, how to improve the quality of choosing versus encouraging the learner to make a specific choice" (Mezirow,1983).

Summary

Learner-managed-learning, rather than mere ideological preference, is now gaining significant ground, particularly at higher education level with educators, employers and with major national initiatives such as EHE and the RSA's Higher Education for Capability scheme. A more androgogical approach to teaching and learning methods is beginning to be viewed as instrumental in promoting qualities and attributes in the learner to ensure that they will become possessors of sound knowledge, confident in their own ability, competent at working with others and capable of initiating and implementing effective action - in short, "enterprising". The growing use of Learning Contracts within higher education is testimony to the value of introducing a mechanism that ensures flexibility, student ownership, accountability and public confidence.

REFERENCES

Department of Employment(1991), "Enterprise in Higher Education: Key Features of Enterprise in Higher Education" London

Knowles M S(1990), The Adult Learner: A Neglected Species. 4th Ed, Gulf Publications, Texas

Mezirow J(1983), A Critical Theory of Adult Learning and Education, in Adult Learning and Education, Tight M(Ed) Routledge & Open University, London

National Foundation for Educational Research(1991), Enterprise in Higher Education: Final Report, NFER, Slough

RSA Higher Education for Capability(1991), Update 7,May 1991

CHAPTER 4

DEVELOPMENT TRAINING

by

K B Everard

Introduction

I first became involved with development training in 1966 when, as a Division Education and Training Manager in ICI, I was responsible for an apprentice school and a secretarial training school. We used to send our apprentices and young secretaries to the YMCA National Centre in the Lake District, for what was then called `character training' - a term no longer in common currency. We now call this experience `development training'. It was pioneered by Outward Bound and Brathay Hall from 1946, as a means of helping young people to mature into adults and to contribute more constructively to their work, home, community and society in general; and its use has steadily grown until the five DTAG organisations alone (Brathay, Outward Bound and Lindley Educational Trusts, Endeavour Training and the YMCA) take about 30,000 young people on their courses every year, quite apart from the adults who come mainly for management and supervisory training. The Royal Society of Arts (Education for Capability) is a corresponding member of the DTAG consortium; Project Trident and the National Association for Outdoor Education are associate members.

What is Development Training?

Development training is an approach to learning, a process of learning, embodying a distinctive philosophy. It combines the concept of *development* - change and growth achieved through learning from experience - with that of *training* - learning specific competences for clear and identifiable purposes. It is invariably based on experiential learning (the Kolb learning cycle: figure 4.1)(Kolb, 1984) , with particular emphasis on the review stage.

Usually a group carries out some task then, with the help of a facilitator, articulates and reflects on this experience, reviewing how they worked together, then drawing conclusions and applying these to future tasks or to their life experiences elsewhere.

Such learning experiences often take place out-of-doors, such as orienteering, rock-climbing, canoeing, sailing and other physical pursuits, but is is equally possible to use indoor activities and community involvement as vehicles for active learning, and to carry out development training in city areas as well as in the country. More can be achieved in a given time when people live together in a sharing community for a while. Although it is sometimes thought to be tough and spartan, this is a misconception; but there is always some element of risk, adventure or challenge, since this enables a person to discover just what he or she can do.

Fig 4.1 THE KOLB LEARNING CYCLE

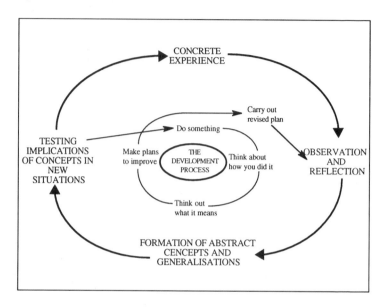

The second major feature of development training is that it is aimed at the systematic and purposeful development of the whole person. It enhances personal effectiveness by evoking a sense of purpose, a set of general coping and learning skills and a degree of self-understanding. The dimensions of personal development along which it operates are shown in figure 4.2.

Whereas the traditional school and university experience is biassed towards knowledge and understanding (cognitive learning), and to a lesser extent capability and skills, development training is particularly strong in the areas of awareness, feelings, motivation, action, beliefs and attitudes (affective learning), although the approach is really holistic rather than compartmentalised.

The values area is particularly challenging for the trainer, because the danger of indoctrination must be averted; however it is an explicit part of the DTAG Code of Practice that values are intentionally transmitted or shaped, including political and religious tolerance, mutual respect, a belief in the dignity and importance of every single person, irrespective of status, age, sex, origin or preconceived contribution to society, and a belief in every individual's capability to learn and go on learning. Indeed, it is a fundamental belief of development trainers that people can and should be encouraged to manage their own learning.

This picture of `whole person development' is similar to one of Plato's definitions of education: `the simultaneous and harmonious development of all aspects of the growing personality'. It is also consistent with the purpose of the school curriculum in England and Wales, as enshrined in clause 1 of the 1988 Education Reform Act: `... (a) promotes the spiritual, moral, cultural, mental and physical development of pupils and of society and (b) prepares such pupils for the opportunities, responsibilities and experiences of adult life'. The words *and of society* are significant, for the follow-up to development training courses is very much involved with its application in the community from which the young people come.

Fig 4.2 DIMENSIONS OF PERSONAL DEVELOPMENT

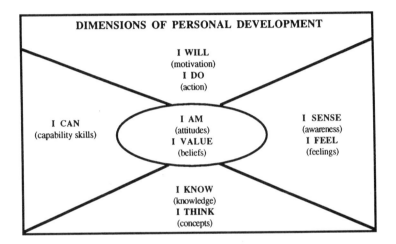

Learning experiences in development training are characterised by: optimistic expectations of the trainees; a strong element of challenge, adventure and risk (more apparent than real, for considerations of physical and emotional safety are paramount); a wide variety of often novel activities; and flexibility in response to an immediate learning need or opportunity. While at first the trainer may intervene in the group process to facilitate learning, after a few days of a week's course, the group will often be given sole responsibility for managing their own learning for much of the time (eg an unaccompanied night expedition).

Development training is used for young and old, community and organisation development as well as personal development, for broad purposes (eg developing potential) or specific targets (eg building a particular management team); it can be indoors or outdoors, residential or non-residential.

Outcomes

The kinds of qualities that may be enhanced by development training are shown in figure 4.3.

Fig 4.3 QUALITIES ENHANCED BY DEVELOPMENT TRAINING

DEVELOPMENT OF

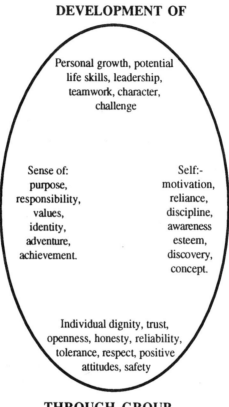

Personal growth, potential
life skills, leadership,
teamwork, character,
challenge

Sense of:
purpose,
responsibility,
values,
identity,
adventure,
achievement.

Self:-
motivation,
reliance,
discipline,
awareness
esteem,
discovery,
concept.

Individual dignity, trust,
openness, honesty, reliability,
tolerance, respect, positive
attitudes, safety

THROUGH GROUP
ACTIVITIES

Although not every individual will manifest changes in every particular, some change in some particular is likely to be discernible in each member of a group. Springett has reviewed the prior research into the outcomes of development training and himself conducted some research, mainly with trainees from the UK woollen industry. Using Rosenberg's self-esteem scale, the general health questionnaire and his own measures of teamwork skills and work attitudes, he reported significant improvements, especially in teamwork and self-esteem. He concluded: `The results as a whole suggest that development training, as its proponents claim, has an important role to play in the building of a positive and effective workforce'(Springett, 1987). He might well have added 'and community', for the same results are likely to be found with trainees who do not belong to a workforce.

Related Approaches

There are many similarities, but also some differences, between development
training and some other approaches to learner-managed, or learner-negotiated,
learning. Figure 4.4 summarises these, but there are other labels. Life and social

Figure 4.4 <u>RELATED APPROACHES</u>

		Possible Differences
I N C R E A S I N G A G E O F L E A R N E R	EDUCATION FOR CAPABILITY	Skills bias. Underplays values, personal qualities, risk.
	LIFE AND SOCIAL SKILLS TRAINING	Underplays challenge, risk, motivation.
	ACTIVE TUTORIAL WORK	Learner has less responsibility for own learning.
	OUTDOOR PURSUITS	Not whole person.
	TVEI	
	ENTERPRISE TRAINING	Strong socio-economic aims. May lack 'moral' component.
	COVERDALE TRAINING	Strong behavioural focus. Not aimed at inner qualities.
	LEADERSHIP TRAINING	Elitist overtones.
	ORGANISATIONAL DEVELOPMENT	Organisational focus.

skills training is a synonym for what UK schools call `personal and social education'. Outdoor pursuits are sometimes called adventure education or outdoor education, though these terms are not quite the same. TVEI (Training and Vocational Education Initiative) takes different forms in different schools, with more or less vocational bias, but always with a less didactic approach than the traditional pedagogy. Enterprise training, as funded by the Training Agency, is aimed at wealth generation, but it may also be used to describe training aimed at developing self-reliance.

Coverdale training, which is based on indoor tasks, has been widely used in British industry since the 1960s and is increasingly used in schools; so far 22 local education authorities have engaged the Coverdale Organisation as consultants, and some impressive results have been achieved, both with pupils down to ten years old and with management and administrative staff in LEAs. Leadership training (Adair's Action-centred Leadership model) has also been widely used in industry, as in the uniformed services, and to some extent in the independent sector of education; it makes use of similar tasks to those used in development training

There is an overlap with organisation development (OD), where the facilitation is also process-based, and strong emphasis placed on learner-managed-learning. Sometimes development training for an individual is used to stimulate community development back-home; there have been several projects, such as Outward bound's `City Challenge' and Brathay's work in Knowsley, which are aimed at improving the quality of community life.

A distinction that should be firmly made is that between training systematically aimed at personal growth, which uses outdoor activities as a vehicle for learning, and outdoor pursuits of a recreational nature, which characterises some types of school trip. Outdoor, residential and adventure activities *per se* do not necessarily lead to significant personal development. Personal growth and maturation, and team-building, have to be competently facilitated, and that is where the tutors' skill is indispensable. The reputable providers devote close attention to the selection and training of their staff, because they have a vital interest in ensuring that development training is effective and continues to enjoy a high reputation.

Some Applications

Development training has many clients and sponsors. The major companies in the UK use it in their staff development programmes, and for building management teams; for example, ICI use Outward Bound courses as the first stage in their management development programme, and the senior project team that developed the new Austin-Rover K-series engine all took part in a week's development training course in the Lake district. The Shell Annual Report for 1986 reported `more emphasis on development training to strengthen managerial ability'.

The Home Office has used it for rehabilitation of offenders and treatment of young persons at risk. It has been used as an alternative to custodial sentencing. Two local authorities have had their senior executives on a team-building exercise outdoors, based on development training methods. It is recommended by the Local Government Training Board. Everard has used it in the management training of over 100 experienced head teachers. A summary of applications is given in figure 4.5.

Fig 4.5 <u>SOME APPLICATIONS OF DEVELOPMENT TRAINING</u>

GENERALLY ENHANCING PERSONAL QUALITIES AND EFFECTIVENESS

PREVENTIVE CARE (eg SCHOOLS OUTREACH)

REHABILITATING YOUNG OFFENDERS

DEVELOPING COMMUNITY LEADERSHIP

EMPOWERING THE DEPRIVED OR INADEQUATE

FOSTERING AN ENTERPRISE CULTURE

ENHANCING QUALITY OF WORKING LIFE

BUILDING MANAGEMENT TEAMS

LOWERING ORGANISATIONAL BARRIERS

(For further worked examples, see Everard(1987)).

The Future

The growth in the number of young people receiving some form of development training in the UK has been striking; a recent survey by Roger Putnam, reported in a book edited by Lord Hunt(1989) is worth reading, and the evidence it presents is being used to persuade government to promote even wider opportunities for young people.

There has been a huge expansion in the number of providers - from single figures to 79 in Cumbria within a decade. New youth service educational support grants and active sponsorship by the Sports Council have helped growth, particularly in urban areas.

The potential for development training in higher education has been discussed by Everard (`Educational Change and Development', 1989, Vol.10, no.1, p.2). It is already used in conjunction with business school programmes. It could be linked to the Training Agency's `Enterprise in Higher Education' programme, and the RSA's Education for Capability in Higher Education initiative.

Thus there is evidence of considerable undeveloped potential in this type of learner-managed experiential learning. One of the few major markets so far uncolonised is the civil service.

The first international conference on learner-managed learning has offered a rare opportunity for those involved with more traditional forms of education to explore the potential and application of development training. Too few such opportunities exist for teachers and trainers to meet and compare notes. They have much to learn from each other, for education and training are really a seamless robe, called learning.

REFERENCES

Everard K B(Ed)(1987) <u>Development Training-Progress and Prospects</u>, BACIE

Hunt Lord(Ed)(1989) <u>In Search of Adventure</u>, Talbot-Adair

Kolb D A (1984) <u>Experiential Learning</u>, Prentice Hall

Springett (1987) <u>The Evaluation of Development Training Courses</u>, Unpublished MSc thesis, University of Sheffield

CHAPTER 5

MAKING WORK RELATED LEARNING COUNT

By

Cathy Hull

The Background and General Approach

There is a growing body of evidence to support the notion that individuals develop their work related learning from a wide variety of informal learning situations in both their working and non-working lives. Until recently, however, there has been little perceived need to take this informal or experiential learning into serious account in the work context. Whilst educators and employers have readily paid lip service to the importance of experiential learning, in practice it has long remained undervalued in a host of ways, not only by employers but, as significantly, by employees themselves.

But in recent years, with the demand for labour increasing as a result of economic and demographic change, employers have been forced to look more closely at strategies for retaining, retraining and redeploying their existing staff. They are having to make the most of their most important resource - the staff they already have. In this respect, they have come to recognise that they can make better plans for the future if they know what their employees have already accomplished and are already capable of - whether these accomplishments and skills were acquired at work or not. In short, there has been a growing recognition that effective training and retraining programmes should in practice, rather than just in theory, "start where the employees are" and take full account of the broad range of their informal experiential learning.

With this in mind a research project was established in 1988. Its aims were two-fold.

** Firstly, to evaluate the extent to which informal experiential learning contributes to an individual employee's performance of his/her everyday job tasks

and

** Secondly, to identify the ways in which the assessment of informal learning can be incorporated into staff development and training programmes as well as staff recruitment strategies

This chapter is primarily concerned with the findings of the first part of the project. A second report, including a set of assessment materials produced by the project is currently being prepared.

The project focussed on how employees acquired their work related learning:

How much learning was the result of formal educational

or training activities, and how much was acquired "on the job" or outside work?

When did, and does, that learning occur?

How far does the employer recognise the extent of the experiential learning acquired by individual employees?

How far does the employer actually know what an individual employee's job involves and the skills required for that job?

The project sought to tackle these questions by extensive, in-depth and structured interviews with employees.

The central aim of these interviews was to take each individual through a careful process of reflection in order to identify the range and extent of their past learning. The interviews were carried out over a six month period with a number of self-selected staff from a broad range of jobs including:-

> **Trainees from a graduate entry scheme with four years' prior work experience**
>
> **Someone from the Youth Training Scheme**
>
> **Several secretarial staff**
>
> **Several clerical staff**
>
> **Branch and Regional Managers**
>
> **Regional Training Managers**
>
> **An Area Manager**
>
> **A senior Personnel Officer**
>
> **Several staff with many years**
>
> **experience at management level,**
>
> **but with no formal qualifications.**

The length and time of each interview varied enormously according to each employee. Some staff, particularly junior staff and those on YTS, needed to be given confidence and encouraged to talk about themselves as employees and as learners. But once started all interviewees soon opened up, often surprising themselves with how much they had to say. As one interviewee put it:

> "Nobody has ever asked me about my job before. I didn't think I would have anything to say to you when I came in. I haven't talked about what I do - not even to myself! But I haven't stopped talking since the word "GO".

Interviewing: the first stage - identification of tasks and responsibilities

The first stage of the interviewing process was concerned with encouraging the employee to develop a detailed and comprehensive analysis of his or her everyday working life. The aim was not only to identify the formally recognised work, but also to take account of those tasks, responsibilities and activities which did not figure in their job descriptions.

Each person chose to approach the task in a different way. So, for example, some found it useful to write down in a structured way their past employment history and formal qualifications. From this, they then used the interview to reflect on what they had written down and, more importantly, what they had left out. Others, by contrast, found it useful to set themselves questions to simply think about in advance of the interview. So, one interviewee said:

> "I have thought about my job and my employment history
>
> non-stop over the past week, in between doing my job; over the washing up and doing the shopping. I found it very valuable. I didn't realise I did so much".

And, indeed, the majority of interviewees were surprised by the extent and breadth of their work.

So, for example, one interviewee initially described her job as a cashier/supervisor as follows:

> "- cashier relief
> - foreign currency
>
> - withdrawals
> - change of name entries
>
> - change of ownership
> - deaths
>
> - data entry
> - collateral charge
>
> - general wordprocessing"

Through reflection the following duties were added to the list:

> "- supervising two other members of staff; this includes receiving all the duties for jobs relating to customer accounts and delegating work
>
> - training new staff on technical equipment; customer services and all general procedures of the organisation
>
> - responsibility for two staff, including handling personal as well as work related problems
>
> - decision making
>
> - customer relations
>
> - handling difficult customers and staff
>
> - talking to a range of staff and customers at all levels
>
> - reading through old legal documents,letters etc.
>
> - assuming tasks from all other departments as necessary, and at regular intervals."

What was particularly significant from this exercise was the extent to which employees assume tasks that are clearly fundamental to the smooth running of the organisation. However, because they are tasks which are not given formal recognition within a job description, they often go unnoticed by employer and employee alike. This in turn means that valuable skills and knowledge are overlooked, under-developed and consequently remain under-utilised by the organisation.

So, one employee said:

> "I've never thought I was much good with people, but now I realise that I am. I can see that a lot of my job involves talking, listening and counselling a lot of different people: customers, colleagues and others. When I look at my experience I realise that I have a lot of knowledge of personnel. And I've always wanted to go into personnel, but didn't think I could do anything. I think now, I would be well placed to go on a training course in personnel management, don't you?"

Interviewing: the second stage - identifying learning sources and sites

Having established the skills required and acquired in the actual performance of his or her job, the next stage of the interviewing process focussed on how and where the employee's learning has occurred. The initial stage of interviewing had already established that their work-related learning was derived from a complex variety of sources and experiences. To make sense of this mass of information, learning sources and sites were broken into four main categories as follows:

A) FORMAL COURSES OR STUDY

> This included school and college-based learning, Open University and other courses which involve rigorous assessment procedures leading to recognised examinations (whether or not the individual actually completed the course or fully qualified).

B) COMPANY TRAINING

> This category included short courses, residential and non-residential courses, open and distance learning, and that training which occurred either on-the-job, at the company training centre, or at another institution. It also included training with present and previous employers.

C) PERSONAL STUDY

> This category referred to any study undertaken by the employee that either related to specific or general job tasks as well as non-work specific learning such as attending an adult education class. Some of this study might have led to formal qualifications - either sector or non-sector specific.

D) INFORMAL (EXPERIENTIAL) LEARNING

> This referred to all other learning the interviewee identified.
> In particular, it referred to learning acquired from life and
> social situations such as bringing up children, voluntary work,
> leisure activities etc.

The two categories that particularly emerged as important sources of learning at this
stage of the interviewing process were: C) <u>PERSONAL STUDY</u> and D)
<u>INFORMAL (EXPERIENTIAL) LEARNING</u>. Take, for example, the case of a
Senior Personnel Manager. This interviewee has a few school-based qualifications.
She has, however, no qualification in Personnel. She identified the learning she
needed in order to carry out responsible management tasks from a wide variety of
informal sources. So, when asked where she had acquired her in-depth knowledge
of employment law she said:-

> "Reading journals. Taking this information apart and
> applying it to this company. I learned a lot about employment
> law when I was on the executive of the Union. You also learn
> a lot about ways of solving problems as well as other
> management skills. Because Unions are always posing or
> facing change for their members, I found that, having to sit on
> their executive, I began to work in that way myself. I began
> to work out ways of improving things from the other side as
> well. I think because I learned a lot more about Unions and
> why they act the way they do and what they are trying to
> achieve, I began to look at things from a wider perspective.
>
> A consequence of all this is that one of my strengths is I do
> have the ability to see through a problem for what it is. I
> think I have always been like that - right back to when I was
> on the debating society of my school.
>
> I also learned a lot from my husband because he is in a
> similar job in the financial sector. We spend time discussing,
> thinking things through and talking."

The interviewee went on to identify other areas of learning from home and life
situations, together with previous jobs held both outside and within the
organisation:

> "For most of the problem solving skills, I have learned
> through probing. I want to know everything. I need to know
> and acquire more information. When people are coming to me
> for help I cannot afford to just jump in and have a go - try
> some hairbrain idea out. You can't afford to make that kind
> of mistake. I need to read, think, look and watch, then advise
> and THEN have a go.
>
> Some of these skills go as far back in my childhood to when I
> worked in an old people's home as a Saturday weekend
> helper. Listening to old folks, you have to LISTEN - actively
> LISTEN so that you can respond, ask them things. Otherwise

they won't ask you back again. I've simply developed this
facility over the years.

People are what really matter. Managers need help to manage
people. Seeing good and bad practice as an employee as well
as a manager and as an adviser has certainly helped.

I have learned knowledge of management partly from
experience; partly; from observation; through talking to
staff, listening, absorbing, reading literature.

I LEARN ALL THE TIME. For example, part of my work is
project research. I might be asked to research into a new
evaluation scheme to be introduced. I read, listen to what
people say, read technical stuff. I take it to the farthest point.
I really love research - finding out more and more about one
thing. Bouncing ideas off other people..."

Many of the interviewees identified family and friends in particular as sources of all
kinds of different types of learning. One interviewee spoke of how the need to
advise her family on financial matters meant that she was determined to give first
rate advice. So, she did all kinds of background reading. Moreover, she said this
also "worked the other way as well", for understanding the feelings of her own
family situtation, had informed and developed her role of counselling and advising
customers through emotional upheaval (death, divorce etc).

Indeed what emerged from all the interviews was the way learning in working and
non-working life constantly interwove in a complex and often very effective
manner. One interviewee, for instance, spoke of going to evening classes to learn a
language as a result of having responsibility for foreign currency at work. In turn,
this resulted in her developing an interest in foreign affairs which she was able to
bring to bear and use to develop her current job.

"When I first started on foreign currency we only dealt with a
few countries. But I've built this up. I think it's because I
began watching the news and holiday programmes and I
realised the news is about all the countries I deal with. It
became so interesting. When I began here, I didn't know
where a Yen or a Franc came from. Now I do. I'm much
more confident when I go on holiday. But watching the news
etc. certainly developed my interest. Work and home are
closely connected here, aren't they?!"

Another interviewee spoke of how teaching a keep-fit class for the local; adult
education centre had altered her working life:

"Supervising is similar to teaching - you need to be
supportive and motivate people. I've never had any training
to supervise but through my evening class, I have developed.
I was even asked to do some training on a training course! I
was terrified and didn't sleep all night. But, for someone who
hadn't been trained there is an irony there! Everyone seemed
pleased with what I did in the training sessions. I was, too,

**But if felt even better when I got my piece
of paper telling me I had passed my keep-fit
teaching exams!"**

Sadly, this remark also typifies the majority of interviewees' attitudes towards their own experiential learning. Whilst acknowledging its existence, it is only when learning is given external recognition, particularly in the form of certification, that it is awarded full value by the individual.

Another interviewee identified the following sources from which she had learned how to operate a computer:

" - previous working life

- colleagues (both formally and informally)

- family and friends

- reading manuals

- trial and error

- reading computer journals

- evening classes "

Significantly, this particular employee now has the key remit for training staff in computing for her company despite never having attended a recognised training course or undertaken any formal examinations. She described her learning like this:

"I joined the company as a comptometer operator. After working in several departments, the General Manager asked me to become his secretary, even though I could not type. I thought a secretary should really be able to type. So I bought a second-hand manual typewriter and taught myself to type. I read the manual. I learned at home. It takes too long at evening classes. I persevered. I got a lot of help from family and friends."

She then began to type but quickly realised that a wordprocessor provides a much lighter keyboard and would be quicker. So she convinced her boss to buy a small PCW. She learned how to use it by:

" - talking to colleagues at work

- reading the manual

- having a go

- family and friends

- reading journals

- watching others "

Having mastered it, she then persuaded her boss to install more complicated equipment and, through the same process of informal learning, became competent.

As a result, she had advised and helped install computers in the company and as previously noted she now has a remit for training others - all of which has been achieved without any formal training of any kind. This is far more typically the case than is generally recognised and applies at all levels of employment from the most junior to the most senior.

In essence this employee had learned how to learn for herself by being both self-directed and self-motivated.

When asked how she learned some of her interpersonal skills she said:

> "Most of my communication skills I learned from my father.
> "Treat people as you would like to be treated", that is what he
> always said. He taught us from a very early age to be happy
> and to work out ways of being happy. I have always
> remembered that. I think it is important to be happy at work.
> So I listen to people, just as my father used to listen to me
> when I was upset. Most people just need to be listened to and
> taken seriously, and they then begin to work out ways of
> coping themselves. My father used to say, working out what
> makes you happy is the hardest thing; obtaining it is much
> easier. All I do is get people to think about what makes them
> happy at work. To think about their own needs at work..."

So, a simple home-spun philosophy has been developed here and transferred to carry out complicated work within a company. In planning training programmes and assessing the potentialities of their staff, employers should begin by understanding the skills and capabilities which employees have rather than just assume that these can be deduced from either their formal qualifications or from a narrow functional view of their current or past job tasks.

People can and do bring so many successful learning experiences to the workplace whilst at the workplace itself often develop new skills not formally recognised in their job descriptions. An awareness of the informal/experiential learning of their employees can release a vast pool of under-utilised talent in an employer's workforce as well as opening up new opportunities for employees is increasing the likelihood of their retention.

But where does this leave the employees' experience of <u>formal company training</u>?

Interestingly over 95% of the interviewees had undergone some formal training with their present organisation. Yet almost all interviewees found such training less effective than their "on the job" learning and criticised the fact that so much of their formal training did not relate to their actual job tasks or as important, build upon the skills and experience they already had.

As one interviewee put it:

> "I did a supervisor's job for three months before being put on
> a proper course. I went on the course but when I returned it
> wasn't possible to put my new found skills to good use.
> Although courses are available for most jobs they are not
> always available immediately. So, most jobs are therefore
> learned by trial and error, thereby gaining valuable
> experience. But the training courses don't recognise what
> you've learned. They are often boring because you learn

> what you already know. And you don't learn anything new or
> what you might find useful..."

So, on the job learning was described as more appropriate because:

> "I not only learn from my own experience, but being taught
> by other members of staff I have learned from their
> experiences too!"

However, on-the-job learning can also prove limiting and over 70% interviewed saw it as the poor cousin of training:

> "It doesn't make you feel confident or positive and leaves me
> demoted because training isn't taken seriously - or they
> wouldn't do it like that when they spend so much on other
> people's training. And you learn bad things you can't rectify.
> So it's the customer who suffers most by getting bad service
> and in the long run this effects the overall position of the
> company."

As regards personal study well over half of the interviewees had also attended an evening class or taken a formal course that had not been certificated. Most stressed the benefits of education beyond simply getting accreditation for job purposes:

> "Everything is around me to be learned. Having to think
> things through for this interview I am surprised at the extent
> that I have learned things unconsciously. But I am very
> conscious of my learning - my own weaknesses and my need
> to find out more information all the time. I am a prober - I
> want to know everything there is to know. I love
> accumulating information. The more I learn the more I want
> to learn. I want to know everything. Almost to conquer
> everything to be learned. That sounds pompous doesn't it?
> But I love to find out more. From any source.

> Listening to other people, watching how THEY do things,
> reading, thinking about my past similar situations and how I
> coped with a particular situation. How this can teach me
> about what I want to know now. Learning from everywhere!
> Does that sound silly? But it isn't just about the learning I do
> for work, it's something to do with the fact that I learn
> because it's fun and that helps my job I suppose.

In the main this personal study is barely recognised by employers and is invariably undervalued by the employees themselves. Learning in our culture is so frequently associated with formal qualifications that uncertificated learning, which may often involve considerable effort and expertise, is disregarded. As a result a host of skills and knowledge that may be applicable in the workplace can be overlooked.

What emerged most clearly from the interviews was that work-related learning was derived from a multiplicity of sources - both at the workplace and outside work.

All too commonly employers had only a limited functional notion of what their employees' actual work tasks involved. Similarly their company training programmes all too frequently ignored the skills and experiences which their employees already brought to the workplace or had developed in their jobs.

Above all, there was a failure to recognise - on the part of employers and employees alike - that learning can and is infinitely transferable and that the starting point for all staff development should be an active process of reflection on, and evaluation of, what employees actually KNOW, DO and are CAPABLE of.

Learning styles

> "As a result of our hereditary equipment, our particular past life experience, and the demands of our present environment, most of us develop learning styles that emphasize some learning abilities over others. Through socialisation experiences, family, school and work, we come to resolve the conflicts between action and reflection and between immediate experience and detached analysis in characteristic ways."

> (David Kolb "The Learning Style Inventory")

The in-depth interviews conducted for this project demonstrated that individuals do indeed develop a range of learning styles in response to the way they were brought up, to their immediate social environment and to their work situation. Any attempt to recognise and build upon prior learning should not only take account of what has been learnt but also the way the individual has learnt and his or her learning style.

What became apparent from the interviews was that, for the most part, company and in-service training takes little account of their employees' widely differing learning styles. Indeed, most company training either ignores the learning style preferences of its employees or makes assumptions about how they want to learn which may be quite wrong. One interviewee stated that her preferred method of learning was very formal and found training courses particularly difficult "because of their methods of discussion and participation". Significantly she was one of the questionnaire respondents unable to identify one single way in which training courses had been of value to her at any time in her career. Had anyone in the company ever thought to ask this employee how she wanted to learn or what value she derived from her training?

In every case it was clear that work-related learning was a much more complicated process than was acknowledged or understood by either the employers or the employees themselves. One useful way of conceptualising this complex process is suggested by Kolb's learning cycle as shown below (Fig 5.1):

Company training should look at ways of breaking into the learning cycles of individual employees at points appropriate to those individuals. For some employees training based on concrete and practical experience is clearly of most value. For others however, particularly those who bring a great deal of experience to the workplace, training would most profitably encourage reflection, conceptualisation or active experimentation according to the task-related objectives and wider purposes of the training programme.

Fig 5.1 THE LEARNING CYCLE

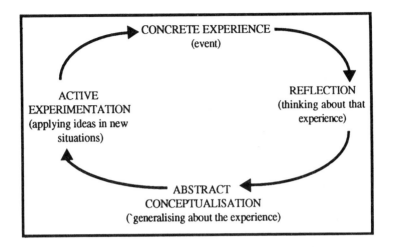

Certainly, it is essential that the starting point in any training should be the employee - their prior learning and their learning styles. In this respect, the very approach of the research project suggested a useful way forward. The structured interviews did successfully illicit a great deal of valuable information both for the employee and the employer.

From the employee's point of view the very fact of being interviewed, although initially daunting, was itself rewarding and self-affirming. One typical response summed up the general feeling:

> "When I came in I wondered what on earth I was going to be able to tell you about myself and what I had learned. I've never met anyone from a university before! I am very shy as a rule as well and I don't like talking to people about myself or my work. I really have enjoyed this though. I have learned a lot about myself today. THANK YOU!"

"Learning a lot about myself" in the positive sense in which this was approached in the structured interviews was, of itself, a great boost to individual confidence. The interviewees learnt <u>from themselves</u> that they had considerable capabilities as learners and as employees, that their jobs were more complicated and involved more skills than even they had appreciated and that they played a significant part in the operations of the organisation. A common remark at the end of the interviews was: "I didn't realise I do so much".

From the employer's point of view a structured interview can make company training and staff development so much more effective by:

1)   identifying more precisely the tasks associated with a particular job which, for a variety of reasons, may go well beyond the formal job specification

2)   identifying and affirming the existing skills and competences of employees

3)   identifying the learning styles most appropriate to particular employees and particularly training tasks

4)   building employees' confidence and morale by affirming what they already know rather than, as is so often the case, making assumptions based on what it is felt the employers do not know.

Much more research is required in the whole area of relating training to individual learning styles and developing means of using an employee's own analysis of his/her training needs in devising appropriate training programmes. Nevertheless, it is clear that training must build upon what employees bring with them to the workplace as well as recognise the skills they have already acquired. Employers must, in short, get to know their staff by encouraging the employees to get to know themselves. Training can then be developed in such a way as to respond to an employee's learning style and be constructed in such a way as to intervene at the appropriate point in the individual's learning cycle:

> "I think I have learned a lot through training courses, and even on the job. But I'm not really sure; nobody has actually asked me before, and I have never thought about it. But I think there is a lot there!"

Conclusions

The research clearly demonstrated that informal experiential learning can and does contribute very significantly to an employee's work performance. However, the extent of the interaction between formal education and training, on the one hand, and informal experiential learning on the other is still under-recognised and under-valued by employees and employers alike. As a result training programmes are frequently less effective than they might be, employees capabilities are often overlooked and resources of all kinds - especially human resources - are being wasted and under-utilised in even those organisations which pride themselves on being efficient.

Much more research needs to be done on how best to take account of experiential learning in training programmes. Nevertheless, this research demonstrated that employers should not make assumptions about what their employees do or do not know or what tasks they do or do not perform in their jobs. All too frequently this is the case, however, and scarce resources are wasted in the provision of training which, for a variety of reasons, is of limited value to the employee. Such costly errors could be avoided if the employer learnt more about his employees by first encouraging the employees to learn and value more about themselves. Even a small scale project of this kind was sufficient to demonstrate the wealth of latent potential which exists in most workforces.

Besides demonstrating that employees bring an enormous amount of experiential learning to the workplace which is all too frequently ignored, the project also highlighted the importance of individual learning styles.

Here again much company training and staff development not only makes assumptions about what their employees know, but also about <u>how</u> their employees learn or prefer to learn. A great deal more in-depth research is required on learning styles, but it is clear that workplace learning is much more complex than most company training assumes. In particular, we need to identify ways in which training programmes can be so developed as to respond to individual learning styles and intervene at appropriate points in an individual's learning cycle. Certainly the structured interview approach on which the project research was based did elicit an enormous amount of valuable information for employer and employee alike.

Learning is a cycle which draws upon experience in all manner of ways. This applies as much to work related learning as to any other kind of learning. Indeed, learning wherever it is acquired informs both working and non-working life in similar proportions. So just as skills and knowledge gained at work can develop an individual's general confidence in his/her non-working life, so also learning outside work can and is frequently used in the working context to considerable effect. If more account were taken of this informal experiential learning by employees and employers, the workplace would not only be more efficient in the sense of realising the full potential of its employees but also, in so doing, become a much more satisfying place to work.

Whilst much more research needs to be done in this area, the importance of informal experiential learning in the work context is now beyond question. Recognising and taking full account of experiential learning presents one of the most significant challenges now facing employers - particularly those operating in a tight labour market such as the banking and finance sector on which this research was based. Correspondingly, educational institutions and research bodies need to spend much more of their time on looking at approaches and mechanisms which will enable not only employers but also individual employees to appreciate the extent and value of their experiential learning.

The failure to recognise the importance of experiential learning results as much from individuals themselves as from their employers. Herein lies the challenge to us all.

CHAPTER 6

USING SYNECTIC PROCESSES IN EDUCATION

By

Richard Dobes and Graham Rawlinson

Background

Managing one's own learning requires a high level of individual responsibility. Such responsibility is accepted by the learner as part of a special relationship between the learner and the teacher. A special relationship with other learners is also needed. Indeed, the learner's peer group may be more influential than the teacher in establishing high levels of commitment and enthusiasm. A central question for educators, therefore, is how do we establish, and then maintain, these special relationships?

.The foundations of Learner-Managed-Learning are created in the very early stages of a child's life. The Harvard Pre-school Project, (White, Kaban and Attanucci, 1979) found that parental style was a key factor in the successful development of independent learning for children in their first two years of life. Intellectual development was highly correlated with the provision of a safe learning environment. Physical safety was important, but so too was intellectual safety, care being taken to reward curiosity and experiment and not to punish it, intentionally or accidentally.

This led to what is described by White et al as the child's ability to "procure the services of others". But the child soon enters a stage of development where the parent as teacher is not dominant. The peer group carries great power in being able to reward or punish, as every nursery teacher is aware. Great skill is needed by nursery staff to create an environment and an ethos, in which the features of successful parenting, noted by White et al can be in evidence amongst the hectic activities of young infants.

By the time the learner enters full time schooling, the reality is that learning feels far from safe. Criticism from peers and all too often from teachers, means that learners are very cautious, only writing or saying what they are sure is acceptable and unlikely to be "punished". Successful learners are the one's who have managed to continue to "procure the services of others" and sampling of child/teacher contact shows that in fact the most able children gain most teacher time, not the least able as may be expected.

Even in Higher Education, in Universities and Colleges, academic staff may find it very difficult to generate an ethos of individual responsibility for learning, of willingness to take risks in learning, the need for security being so strong. Graduates then enter professions and businesses and the same patterns of behaviour continue.

Company management meetings may be dull and formal, dialogue being limited to that which is unchallengeable, protected by agreed role positions of participants. When necessity requires the orthodox to be challenged, meetings may be full of conflict, recriminations and retaliation as each person seeks to expose weaknesses in knowledge or logic of the others.

There is much evidence that this loss of independent learning need not be permanent. At any stage in a person's development, if sufficient care is taken to re-establish a special relationship between teacher and learner and between learner and the learner's peer group, the high levels of commitment, individual responsibility and willingness to innovate will return.

To do this, in education or in work, safe operating procedures are needed. These can be formal and explicit or informal and implicit, but they must be understood and accepted by all parties. When in place, learning is efficient and effective, as learning can occur at the edge of what is known. Rapid learning takes place as a research activity rather than a digestion of safe knowledge, simply the acceptance of given facts.

In companies, decision making and planning becomes a creative and innovative activity, drawing on the resources of all participants, as a team with common goals and in which each individual becomes responsible for their own contribution within the security of the procedures that have been agreed.

In education these procedures are established in the use of project/research based learning, with negotiated "learning contracts", at a simple level for younger children and as written agreements in Higher Education. In companies the ideas of Flat Management, Total Quality Management and now Total Continuous Improvement are attempts to create a holistic approach to company activities, to open up procedures in which each individual can participate and contribute as fully as possible.

The use of Brainstorming and other processes such as the Nominal Group Technique (NGT) provide some of the necessary safety features for creativity. In NGT this is achieved by banning debate while ideas are created and rules are established to protect ideas from tampering or "theft" by others. Synectics processes were developed for companies to take these techniques much further, and proven success of these techniques has led to attempts to develop these techniques for use in education.

Synectics Processes

Synectics is a generic label for a range of techniques, behaviour and meeting structures that have been identified as increasing the probability of success in invention and creative problem-solving. The methods have been established by tape-recording and video-taping several thousand invention and problem-solving sessions over the last 30 years, and by experiment with alternative techniques in a wide variety of situations.

To the extent that the methods have been derived from observation of what people do when they are being successful, they can be considered as `common sense', but they differ markedly from what is considered normal behaviour in a working environment (whether in business, industry, government or elsewhere).

One of the principal differences is that thought processes that normally go on privately, and sometimes subconsciously, are made explicit and public. By sharing formative stages of their thinking and activities, the members of a Synectics group greatly accelerate the discovery of novel connections and solutions.

To do so, Synectics uses the brainstorming principle of suspending judgement, but extends it substantially so that it applies not only to ideas but to problem statements, goals and wishes. Participants are encouraged to abandon the internal censoring or thoughts (which continues out of their conscious awareness even in a brainstorming session) by the use of a range of techniques involving metaphor, analogy, fantasy, visualisation, association etc. The `excursion' techniques provide distance from the problem and open up novel avenues of approach.

When it becomes necessary to reintroduce judgement, Synectics does so in a way that maintains the constructive and emotionally safe climate created in the initial period of ideas and concept generation. Developmental thinking is used to explore ideas which are emotionally attractive, though not yet feasible; all the potentially positive features of the ideas are identified, and the deficiencies are used to give the direction for improvement. In this way the elements of novelty are preserved while the idea is modified to make it feasible. (This process contrasts with conventional screening of ideas into `good' and `bad' after brainstorming, when novel ideas are likely to be screened out because they are not feasible).

To create and maintain the positive environment, the Synectics session will normally be run by a skilled facilitator (`process controller') who takes no part in the content of the meeting. Responsibility for describing the problem, specifying the objectives of the session, selecting the ideas to be developed and evaluating ideas during the development phase is in the hands of the problem owner (`client') defined as the individual with decision-making and action responsibility. When, as in most organisations, more that one individual has some share in the decision-making, the model is extended to accommodate each of the problem-owners, usually one at a time. The subsequent handling of opinions and value judgements, combined with the positive climate, makes Synectics techniques particularly effective for the constructive resolution of conflict.

Many of the elements of the Synectics processes have application outside the formal invention/problem-solving meeting and can be used to develop a working style that is constructive, open-minded, tolerant of diversity and highly co-operative. The culture created in the Synectics meeting can be extended to all the operations of the working group and it is in this kind of environment that innovation flourishes and change is managed productively.

Synectics - the 3 day Course

A charitable company, Synectics Education Initiative, has been set up in the U.K., to "empower creative change in Education by equipping teachers, students, administrators and specialists with enhanced levels of skill in problem-solving, communication and teamwork". A 3-day course is offered to schools, colleges and administrators to provide the essential foundations of Synectics processes so that participants can use them within the education system.

This course is being integrated into an undergraduate engineering course the University of Surrey. It is being well received by staff and students at a personal level, and it is recognised that the graduate engineers, as future managers in industry, will be well placed to contribute to effective management of teams as well as within teams.

The relevance of Synectics processes to Learner Managed Learning is reflected in the Learning Objectives of the course. These are:

1. To understand better how the way you interact with others affects innovation and teamwork.

2. To identify the most appropriate role in a meeting for yourself and others.

3. To view problems in fresh ways.

4. To develop ways of getting new ideas and suggestions.

5. To provide additional ways of listening to ideas and suggestions.

Some parts of the course may seem familiar, for example, the need to find value in ideas and to look for and acknowledge positive features. Other parts are fairly special to the Synectics process. For "In/Out Listening", the participant is encouraged to divide a note pad into two sections, one for the notes we ordinarily make about what is being said, the other to record the ideas that are spontaneously triggered, ideas which are normally lost and yet which may prove to be the most productive.

Participants are guided to:

speak for themselves and let others do the same;

"mind your own business" so that ideas and opinions are given only when wanted;

assume "constructive intent";

understand before evaluating (by paraphrasing what has been said as a check to understanding);

speak for easy listening, by ensuring that they "headline" what they want first and then provide background.

A key element of the course is how negatives are used to give direction to problem solving. By changing a statement that "The problem is ..." to "How do we ..." you encourage a positive attitude to solutions. The workshop in Opava was centred around the facilitation of a problem-solving situation, from which "thinking positively" was warmly received.

The Workshop

Ordinarily, the Innovative Teamwork session has no more than 8 participants so that everyone has a chance to contribute and feel part of the process. However, with 20 participants, mostly Czechoslovakian students and teachers, we decided that after a brief outline of the Synectics processes we would split the group and see how it went, with a chance for feedback at the end. The session was much shorter than really desirable, with just 1.5 hours to establish some practice of the process and some explanation of the content and background. Also, although Richard Dobes was multi-lingual, I realised that I would have to rely on translation, and I wondered how I would cope with the translator's interruptions and the possible difficulty that some concepts might not translate easily.

We spent more time than usual in providing the outline and background. Synectics processes are best understood by going straight into practice with reflection afterwards. Once the practice session started, however, I was soon made aware that Synectics processes are readily understood by all cultures.

As facilitator I will report my session and as participant Norman Graves will report on the session led by Richard Dobes.

Report on Group 1

A "problem solve" in Synectics, starts with the identification of a problem owner. I was the one U.K. participant of my group. The rest of the group were Czechoslovakian students. The problem itself was how to turn an educational journal into a non-loss maker without losing its educational value.

After a slightly hesitant start ideas were generated quietly, interrupted only briefly by the occasional need for translation. As ideas creation slowed down we went into role allocation, where each participant was asked to provide an idea that would come from the role allocated. Roles included a banker, a ship's captain, a market gardener, a newspaper editor, and so on.

The students soon picked up the technique of using the negatives, with guidance from the problem owner on the problems of using the ideas suggested. The negatives became positives, as with statements of "how to steer clear of the rocks" or "how to create a new species of flower".

The humour and goodwill indicated how positively the process was received. Ideas were certainly novel, a sign of success at the first stage of the process. It was unfortunate that the session had to be so short.

Students reported that the session was the most useful in the whole conference, and it was encouraging to see that they could understand that the processes connect well with the concepts of Learner Managed Learning to which they had been exposed. They readily recognised their value in the process of change now going on in the education system in Eastern Europe.

Report on Group 2

Members of Group 2 were asked for a real problem that required to be solved. A participant who was a Czechoslovak with a good command of English suggested a problem which he had been unable to solve, namely the need to convince the Higher Education authorities in the local university that a Business School should be set up. This was accepted by the participants. A brainstorming session then followed in which various suggestions were put forward without comments from anyone and written up on a flipchart.

The group was made up partly of English and Czech speakers and inevitably most of the suggestions came from the English speakers who were more comfortable in both the language and the style of contribution. However most members of the group eventually participated in the exercise.

The next stage was that of combining sugested ideas which had much in common and then highlighting those which, given the known circumstances as indicated by the `problem owner', were most likely to be successful. This led to some lively discussion which unfortunately had to be cut short by the need to close the session.

Perhaps the most useful aspect of the exercise, particularly for those new to it , was the realisation that with an open-ended and positive approach to the solution of problems, the range of ideas obtained was wide and fruitful.

Europe and Beyond

At the end of the conference I had little doubt that Learner Managed Learning has a central place in the development of education in Eastern Europe. I felt that it was necessary to make clear to our Czechoslovakian students that education in Western Europe also has a long way to go in adopting these ideas. Many of the changes relate to the student/teacher relationship. By incorporating Synectics processes, with the emphasis on creative problem solving, teamwork and communication, the student relationship can be changed as well, a necessary development if students really are to manage their own learning. The Synectics Education Initiative is starting to share these processes within the U.K. Flexible delivery seems essential for adoption of the processes in the many very different educational systems for different ages and different cultures and traditions.

Synectics and *Enterprise*

Much of this report attempts to outline why the workshop is relevant to education in the same way it is relevant to the commercial world. As the Synectics processes have been developed in the commercial world, this seems necessary. In the U.K. 56 Higher Education Institutions have been funded by Her Majesty's Government to generate "*Enterprise*" in Higher Education. The interpretation of *Enterprise* has been in terms of the development of student personal skills (at the University of Surrey we concentrate on Problem Solving, Teamwork and Communication) and the idea of partnership in the learning process between staff, students and employers.

The process of Learner-Managed-Learning is best started in the first years of life and developed as a continuum through school, college and into professional working life. If at any stage - pre-school, school, or in work - we lose sight of the value of Learner-Managed-Learning then we are failing ourselves, our learners, and the most needy in the world, who may be some way off receiving the benefits that we, as independent learners, already have.

Less developed countries cannot afford to copy the failings of the education system of the western world. Resources put into education will need to lead to maximum benefits for those countries. Building into the education system the procedures for safe learning is essential, for efficient and effective learning, just as they are essential for the development of competitive company activity.

Note

The release of the use of the Synectics processes owes much to the open thinking of Synectics Ltd, who have provided encouragement, support and "training" very much in the style of Learner Managed Learning.

REFERENCES

Nolan V (1987) The Innovator's Handbook (The Skills of Innovative Management), Sphere Books, London

White BL, Kaban BT and Attanucci JS (1979) The Origins of Human Competence, Laxington Books, U.S.A.

CHAPTER 7

FOSTERING LEARNER-MANAGED-LEARNING IN TEACHER EDUCATION

By

Diane Montgomery

Introduction

Learning something new often presents us with the excitement of challenge and is often an uncomfortable and somewhat incoherent experience. Weil (1990) talked of "going beyond givenness" as just this sort of experience and invited us to think of a learning experience each one of us had had which caused us to be jarred or surprised. One such learning experience I recalled was with my class of '84. I had in consultation with tutors and previous year groups of students decided to include some opportunities for learner-managed-learning into the year 4, B.Ed teacher education students' programme. This was the first time we had had the opportunity to work with them for a whole day.

The programme was called Psychology and Special Needs. It was an option course for students interested in mixed ability teaching in mainstream schools. The programme included:-

* classroom management
* pupils with emotional and behavioural difficulties
* needs of slower learners (pupils with general learning difficulties)
* pupils with specific learning difficulties i.e. reading, spelling,handwriting (dyslexics) and number
* able learners needs
* pupils with physical and sensory difficulties

Opportunity To Practise LML

All students each year opted to study this programme. We had 108 hours <u>contact</u> time which was spread across the year on one day a week for 4 hours in the day with up to 60 students. The window of opportunity came as the resourcing of courses declined so that staff numbers decreased whilst student numbers increased. This resulted in having one full-time member of staff for the day and the assistance of 3 part-time staff for one and a half hours each afternoon. Contact time could not continue to be face-to-face and independent study could be "justified" at last. The following is the structure of each weeks' programme introducing independent study:-

*	09.00 - 09.45	Clinic tutorials
*	10.00 - 11.00	Mass lecture (Cooks' tour of area, issues and structures)

*	11.30 - 12.30	Independent study workshops in collaborative groups
*	02.00 - 03.00	Seminar groups x 4 groups
		(02.00 - 02.30 debriefing from workshops)
		(02.30 - 03.30 discussion of research papers)
*	03.30 - 04.00	Tea and tutorials

The challenge that we also faced was that we were trying to teach students to change from teacher-led and teacher-directed experiences in their own education to more open and experiential learning and ways of working with primary education pupils. To do this using lectures and methods typical of higher education was inconsistent with what we were trying to help the students achieve in the classroom. We wanted them to understand what learners needed to know, do and feel and so needed them to go through some similar learning experiences at their own level. It became apparent that we could not lecture it into their framework of understanding.

On the one hand we were teaching them that pupils in schools need opportunities to learn by doing but we were not always transferring this knowledge to the students' situation, a justifiable cause for complaint when we showed them the following. Estimates of learning achieved in various modes:-

* 10 per cent of what we read

* 20 per cent of what we hear

* 30 per cent of what we see

* 50 per cent of what we see and hear

* 80 per cent of what <u>we</u> say

* 90 per cent of what we <u>say and do at the same time</u>

Problems

The jarring experience came when this carefully thought out programme was implemented. A vivid example was on a particular Thursday. The theme for the day was <u>Early Screening Techniques</u> to identify learning difficulties. The mass lecture expanded types of screening and the nature and quality screening instruments used in local LEA's. At 11.30 the students assembled in their four workshop rooms and were set to work in self-organised, and self-selected groups of 2 and 3 on the screening instruments and tests which we had set out for the study. The workshop task was for them to work through the test instruments to identify those they thought were good and try to identify why they thought so. Each group had a similar selection of 5 test instruments.

Within 20 minutes each workshop had been depleted of half its members. They had "finished". Of the rest, one small group went on working for $1\frac{1}{2}$ to 2 hours which was our estimated "real" time for the job, the rest exited promptly at 12.30 task uncompleted.

We discovered that many of the students had just flipped through the instruments, made one or two comments agreed these and went off to do their "important" personal tasks. In the debriefing in the afternoon we discovered many problems. Their previous learning history at school and then at college had given them "learned helplessness" in this situation. They had little motivation to seek education in the psychopedagogy programme without our direction.

Analysis

Their learning had been a <u>cycle of disconnections</u> (Fig 7.1) which we needed to reconnect, transfer and change in order to help them find interest and pleasure in learning for its own sake. They were used to being corralled and policed. We learnt much in the debriefing sessions about the feelings, wants, needs and the people we were trying to teach. All of which had to be catered for in our plan if their learning was to be facilitated.

Fig 7.1 A CYCLE OF DISCONNECTIONS

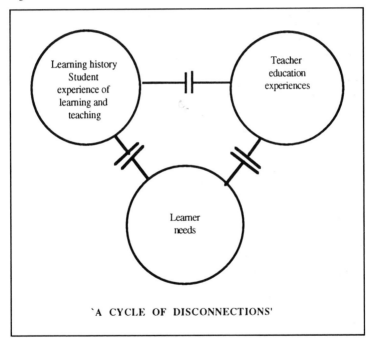

Over the first few weeks our debriefing sessions revealed their feelings of:

      * desertion

      * abandonment

      * anger

      * fear

* frustration

* anxiety

They projected these angers and fears outwards upon us. They felt we were abandoning them. They were angry when they felt they had not done the work properly or had got some "wrong" answers. They blamed us for not explaining carefully enough what they were to do and exactly how they should do it and the results they should expect.

The debriefing was very important it allowed them to release these pent up emotions and enabled us to judge whether it was best to reset an experience or move on. In these sessions the students constructed for themselves cognitive scripts (Anderson 1980) to help them organise their learning.

Results

This programme of self-directed learning took place in their fourth year, not our choice, but where we were allowed to operate in the programme. Of course this should have been part of their first year BEd learning experiences. It took just over a term and a half for our objectives and theirs to be realised.

After about a term and a half each year the vast majority became confident and self-organised and the absolute joy came when they began to organise us and take control of the programme by defining their own needs. They opted in and out of the programme on a rational basis which they felt able to tell us about. They made up any perceived lost time without our encouragement to do so but because they had mapped out their needs, and they began to question the basis of our assumptions about theory, practice and method. They told us of research papers which they had read which were more recent or relevant than the ones we suggested they might read. The last few months of the course were extremely pleasurable and stimulating. The large majority of students prepared themselves so well they lost their fear of the final exams and many looked forward to them as an opportunity to show what they knew. In the last term they not only organised themselves they organised us and determined the lecture and seminar programme and speakers they wished to hear. Interspersed with the regular programme during the last term and a half they were asked to organise a day's teaching and learning for the rest of the group from the vantage point of a curricular specialism they were studying e.g. Reading, Mathematics or PE. These groups were given a few research papers to start them off and they organised teaching and learning for the rest of us on reading difficulties, number difficulties and the difficulties and needs of clumsy children or on handwriting problems.

It has frequently been observed that the best way to learn anything is to try to teach it to someone else and this had often been used in the programme as a teaching and learning format as well as with pupils in schools. These approaches were also particularly successful from the point of view of the students' learning.

Staff Reactions and Staff Development

The staff however often felt that in sitting quietly and listening they were not doing their job properly and "teaching" the students. It was therefore necessary to ensure that the staff had a debriefing session each day of the programme hence the section entitled "tea and tutorials". Overtly staff met in the refectory for a cup of tea and to be available for students to consult them. Covertly they were there for their own debriefing needs. This session was a most important part of the programme. The time when the students were in the workshop was used for forward planning and designing materials. As indicated not all problems rested with the students learning, colleagues found it hard not to regard the seminar as a mini lecture forum or to organise 2 students to "read the paper" to the rest. Our plan required all students to read the papers and share the main parts from their viewpoint then to work over the paper in a structured way to fill in relevant detail.

Some staff wanted to stop students slipping away from workshops and tried to preside over them giving out notes of key learning points before or after sessions or in the seminars. The desire to create uniformity in learning by this form of intervention was very strong. Hence the need to debrief them and keep the aims and purposes of the programme uppermost in their minds.

To help staff and students organise themselves for self-directed or learner managed learning it was realised that both groups needed to be trained and weaned towards freedom and autonomy if it was to be achieved in our short time table. To do this, ways of developing these shared purposes had to be designed and some of the subskills of LML needed to be uncovered and passed on.

At the same time as working with the students and staff it was equally important that the substance of what they were learning had some coherence and structure. This meant defining for ourselves teaching and learning and "good" teaching and learning. We also needed a secure knowledge base and theoretical framework on which to base this. Since Stones (1979) and Wragg (1984) amongst others have said there is no coherent theory and practice of education this meant that it was necessary to try to formulate a coherent theory and practice of education which would link all aspects of what we are taught, what we did and how we explained it. This approach was termed cognitive - process theory and practice (Montgomery 1989) and some illustrative examples are given in the next section.

Cognitive-Process Learning

In doing this it became clear that we were working or trying to operate at three different levels of intellectual operation but all at the same time! This was similar to the levels expressed in Blooms' (1956) Taxonomy of Educational Objectives but ours were shingled on each other.

Mental Operations at 3 Levels (Bloom's Taxonomy 1956)

1)   Acquisition of new content and method material.

2)   Application of education theory and research to the new material

3)   Analysis, synthesis and evaluation of the links between 1) and 2).

Kolb's (1984) experimental learning cycle was too simple a model for our purposes, it was necessary to identify a way of working which suited our students needs and their processes of learning. This was defined as the cognitive - process learning spiral of the "action learner". This fitted with the theoretical model of teaching.

Fig 7.2 <u>COGNITIVE-PROCESS LEARNING SPIRAL</u>

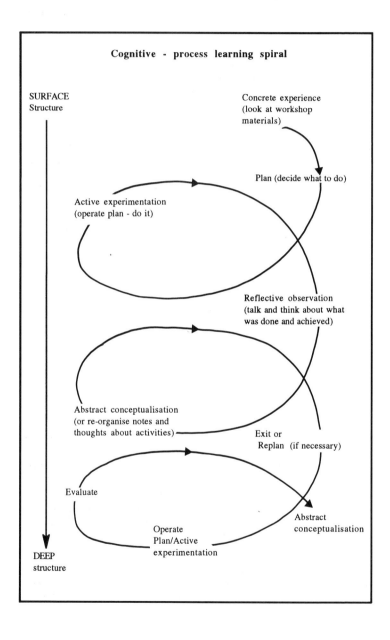

By this process we were trying to help the students move from "surface to a deep" approach to learning (Marton, Housnell & Entwistle 1984).

According to Gibbs (1990) Surface Approaches to learning in Higher Education are characterised by:

1)   a heavy workload

2)   relatively high class contact hours

3)   an excessive amount of course material

4)   a lack of opportunity to pursue subjects in depth

5)   a lack of choice over subjects

6)   a lack of choice over methods of study

7)   a threatening and anxiety provoking assessment system.

Our BEd course qualified one hundred per cent in providing surface learning until we began to change their way of working in our area. What we were unable to do was to change the ways of learning and teaching on the other two thirds of their programme, the students did however transfer some of their learning strategies and made new demands on other teaching teams.

Fostering a deep learning approach according to Gibbs (1990) rests in the obverse of the factors which foster the surface approach for example:-

1)   relatively low class contact hours

2)   intrinsic interest in the subject

3)   freedom in learning in context and method or scope for intellectual independence and additionally

4)   perceived "good" teaching.

Gibbs states that four key elements have been identified in "good" teaching as follows:

1)   motivational context in which motivation is intrinsic and there is a "need" to know and have ownership of it

2)   learner activity - rather than passivity although doing is not enough we have to reflect and correct present with past learning

3)   interaction with others so that ideas can be discussed and negotiated or "taught" by students to others for the best way of learning something is to teach it to someone else

4)   a well-structured knowledge base where the structure is displayed and integrated into meaningful wholes not disparate units. This is best seen in interdisciplinary studies.

Our programme came at a late stage in the students' learning history in teacher education and it was relatively brief. The students' opinion was that they should have spent the whole of the week within our special needs programme so that they could follow up all the lines of enquiry they had identified for themselves. We were able to establish clear links between their behaviour and the deep learning criteria in relation to motivation, learner activity and interaction with others.

Developing the well-structured knowledge base was not so easy. Instead it seemed more important to develop in the students higher order reading and study skills to handle the huge and disparate base with which they had to deal. Here the cognitive-process pedagogy for helping them organise the way they worked with pupils proved invaluable in helping us work with them. In relation to this we needed to analyse the sub-skills of L.M.L. in higher education and then try to help our students develop these. We found that not only did our learners exhibit "learned helplessness" in the workshops they lacked learning skills in other key areas of our programme such as the ability to take adequate notes in lectures, to organise these notes for later learning and to read with understanding the research papers we offered them. When they were presented with Bloom's (1956) Taxonomy and a set of resource materials to evaluate in relation to the taxonomic levels they were at first incapable of doing so. When given a research paper by Leach (1983) on Early Screening Techniques and asked to draw out the main point and fill in a flow chart (Fig 7.3) of the potential structure of the main and subordinate points of the paper, many found this task almost impossible.

Fig 7.3   <u>EXAMPLE OF THE FLOW STRUCTURE GIVEN</u>

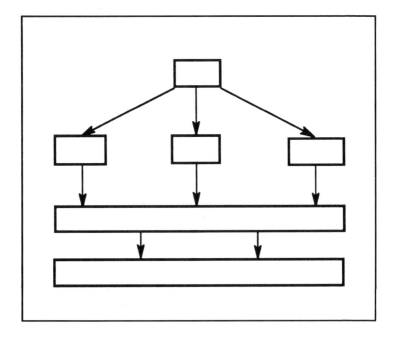

Learning Skills Required

In reading research papers in general they demonstrated an inability to infer the basic organising principles and to criticise constraints and methodology. This was mainly because their reading strategies were ineffective. They expected to understand a paper by reading it through several times or once if they were short of time. Others expected to understand it by reading and making short notes so reproducing the paper in summary form.

Both these techniques were found to be ineffective as reading strategies for complex text (Thomas and Harri-Augstein 1984). The note taking read only enabled facts to be recalled rather than understanding the whole to be achieved. Our students needed to learn how to become <u>reflective</u> readers so that they could get the maximum benefit from unguided and independent learning. This was a key subskill needed by the autonomous learner. Practice in learning to read papers for the main point, their basic substructures and meaning flow quickly proved an effective strategy. The students complained that trying to solve the flow chart problem took them hours and hours of thought and study but they found it compelling to pursue. We had found a way of getting them to contribute a more than equal amount of their own time to the study programme. This is usually a hypothetical contribution in most students cases. As the students became competent readers and developed learning "scripts" (Anderson 1980) to deal with new learning experiences they began to reject other areas of the course in which they were "spoon fed".

The cognitive study skills we worked on at the students' level we also illustrated at the pupils' level. Some examples of the types of cognitive study skills worked upon:-

* Locating the main and subordinate points

* Flow charting

* Labelling

* Deletion

* Categorising

* Tabulating

* Comparing

* Sequencing

* Contrasting

* Classifying

* Drafting and redrafting

* Diagramming

* Critical appreciation

* Identification of intent, bias, attitude, tone, propaganda

The view of good teaching which was made explicit to the students was as follows:-

"Good teaching is occurring where students learn most of
what the teachers intended and much more beside, where they

> continue to study and pursue the topic long after the lesson
> ends, where they do not have to be made to work but want to
> do so. Good teaching motivates students to learn."

The essentials of teaching suggested were that when you <u>teach</u> something it automatically carries with it the assumption that the learners have learned or are learning it. The implications of this are that:-

* telling is not teaching

* lecturing is not teaching

for when you tell pupils information you cannot assume that they learn it. To lecture is a very poor teaching device in this respect and leads one to question seriously the 2 and 3 hour lectures often given in Higher Education courses by lecturers. As these lecturers do not need to be trained teachers it is perhaps not surprising they have not addressed these issues. They also seem to make the assumption that their students are autonomous learners and as can be shown this is seldom the case. Thus much of what students acquire as information is non-transferable and their intellectual skills remain undeveloped even after a degree programme. There are of course a small proportion of students who are "<u>able</u>" learners the rest can be helped to become so.

Some key attributes of able learners, according to Freeman (1985),are:

* self organised learners

* autonomous learners

* profit without help from their own experiences

 Thomas and Harri-Augstein (1984) suggest that able learners hold "learning conversations" with themselves.

In contrast they suggest that slower learners are in "<u>robot</u>" mode and can only operate old and well tried learning routine. Span (1988) suggests that most learners need help to tap into their meta cognitive events if they are to become able learners. It was this aspect that we were trying to work on with our students for a large part of the debriefing sessions, the tutorials and the discussion of the research papers concentrated upon the ways in which the students understanding had been achieved and what learning strategies they had achieved. Once they had made these explicit it was possible for them on other occasions to observe and reflect independently upon these meta cognitions.

The cognitive process pedagogy determined two central objectives in teaching (Montgomery 1981)

* to enable pupils to think effectively and

* to express those thoughts succinctly in a variety of modes

Four main methods of achieving these objectives with pupils in schools and students in higher and further education were refined as follows:-

1) Investigative, problem-finding and problem solving and resolving approaches, creative problem

2) Cognitive study skills - higher order cognitive and reading skills

3)   Language experience approaches - particularly collaborative
        learning and conflict management strategies

4)   Games, simulations and role play.

(Examples of these approaches may be found in Montgomery   1990)

Only when we began to practice in HE what we preached for students to do at
school level did we begin to achieve deep learning levels. In this process we learnt
that no amount of independent study could necessarily achieve this. If we wanted
all our students to be enabled to achieve their best we needed to give them some
education in the sub-skills which would facilitate higher order learning. Not all
students bring these skills into HE or learn them there. If we do not help students
learn these sub-skills we discriminate against those whose previous learning
experiences have been limiting and we contain them in a cycle of deprivation.

Epilogue

By the end of the programme our learners had become autonomous, they took
control of their own learning and the programme and wrote their own reports. The
final examination results profile changed from a normal inverted U-shaped
distribution to a marked shift towards the higher degree classifications.
"Uncomfortably high" numbers appeared in the first and upper second class
categories too many for neat administrative purposes, which meant that a whole
new area of debate was opened up within the college.

REFERENCES

Anderson (1980) Cognitive Psychology, Prentice Hall

Bloom B S (1956) A Taxonomy of Educational Objectives, Vol 1

Longman

Freeman J (1985) The Psychology of Gifted Children, John Wiley

Gibbs G (1988) Learning by Doing , F E Unit, DES

Gibbs G (1990) Improving Student Learning Project, Centre for Staff Development,
Oxford Polytechnic/CNAA)

Kolb DA (1984) Experimental Learning - Experience as a Source of Learning and
Development, Prentice Hall

Leach D (1983) Early Screening Procedures, School Psychology
International Vol 4 pp 47-56

Marton F, Hounsell D & Entwistle N(Eds) (1984) The Experience of Learning,
Scottish Academic Press

Montgomery D (1981) Education Comes of Age. The Nature of Modern Teaching,
School Psychology International Vol 1 pp 2-4

Montgomery D (1989) Managing Behaviour Problems, Hodder & Stoughton

Montgomery D (1990) Children with Learning Difficulties, Cassell

Montgomery D & Hadfield N (1989) Practical Teacher Appraisal, Kogan Page

Stones E (1979) Psychopedagogy, Routledge & Kegan Paul

Thomas L (1984) and Harri-Augstein S <u>The Self Organised Learner</u> COPOL Conference, Kingston Polytechnic

Wragg E(1984) <u>Conference Address</u>, Cambridge Institute of Education

Span P (1988)'Intelligence and high ability', <u>Conference Address,9th International Conference,</u> Plovdiv Bulgaria

CHAPTER 8

THE CASE FOR LEARNER-MANAGED-LEARNING
IN HEALTH PROFESSIONALS' EDUCATION

By

BETTY ANDERSEN

Introduction

In presenting the case for learner-managed-learning in health professionals' education I would like to address four issues, namely:

1) the basis of the claim that learner managed learning makes sense for the education of professional groups such as nurses.

2) the case for varying degrees of learner-managed learning within programmes such as nursing and other professional practices.

3) the implementation of such an approach and finally;

4) the evidence that it works.

The approach adopted by the School of Nursing and Health Studies, University of Western Sydney, Macarthur (UWSM) is commonly referred to as problem-based learning (PBL) though we find it more appropriate to use the term `practice-based'. Because it has self-directedness as one of its main tenets, PBL can be regarded as being consistent with other learner-managed-learning approaches. During the preparation made for this paper (in which learner-managed-learning is illustrated by PBL), two significant factors emerged. If we are to be not too prescriptive in defining LML then it will be recognised that programmes will vary in terms of the nature and extent of the learner-managed aspects. I would like to suggest that programmes which claim to use LML approaches could be described as being at one point or another on four continua, in respect of who manages or controls that aspect of the curriculum, namely:

(1) course organisation

(2) selection of learning experiences

(3) the actual learning process

(4) the assessment process.

Some programmes may be more totally learner-managed than others on any or all of the above four curriculum aspects. What causes any differences to emerge should be carefully examined in the light of the specific type of course and of statutory regulations governing courses leading to professional registration.

The second factor which emerged was, that though I shall confine this discussion largely to the self-directed aspects of PBL, the success of our programme has been due to a totality of factors and not to the self-directed element alone. The effectiveness of the application of the learning approach to the organisation and implementation of the course is attributable to a marked degree to the detailed conceptual framework of the curriculum which reflects the realities of actual nursing practice. The conceptual framework resulted from an extensive analysis of the practice of nursing, including the functions and characteristics of the practitioner needed for the profession to advance into this final decade of the twentieth century and beyond.

The analysis was coupled with performance evaluation research in respect of key behaviours which formed the basis of significant professional nursing functions (Andersen 1976; 1984). The models which resulted from the analysis have been subjected to ongoing testing, review and amplification by faculty in the period between 1985-1989.

Justification for self-directed learning in health professionals' education

The first of the four issues highlighted in this paper raises a very significant question. How can self-directedness be justified in terms of the professional practice of nursing when many colleagues would still insist that all nurses are other-directed? The discussion which follows deliberately addresses the demands made on the professional-level nurse as distinct from those who carry out less responsible and more dependent functions.

A number of justifying reasons can be provided to justify self-directedness in practice and in education for that practice. However I have chosen to focus on the context of practice; its characteristics and the nature of the response required of the nurse to patient situations in that context which in itself provides sufficient justification for self-directedness in practice.

The context of practice has action of one form or another as its basis; it is dynamic in that situations, circumstances and conditions change, often very rapidly; it is invariably complex as many interactive factors combine to determine any one patient/client situation; usually one workplace is made up of a varying number of patients or clients at any one time. Finally, the outcomes of patient-nurse interactions have very direct and often serious consequences for the patient/client.

In this dynamic action context what is the nature of the response demanded of the professional nurse? This question is best answered by reviewing the overall activity of nursing in terms of an amplified enquiry model, figure 8.1 (Andersen 1978, 1989). Clinical judgment is centrally significant in any practice which has as its goal an improvement in the patient situation. The quality of judgment will inevitably influence the quality of intervention initiated and the quality of judgment will in turn be influenced by how knowledge is structured, how data is acquired, recalled, processed and evaluated. The patient situations to which a nurse must respond are not always well defined nor are they exact replicas of those encountered the day before or even an hour before. In some fields of practice a response very often must be immediate with consequences which may be life-threatening in nature.

Fig 8.1 MODEL OF NURSING ACTIVITY

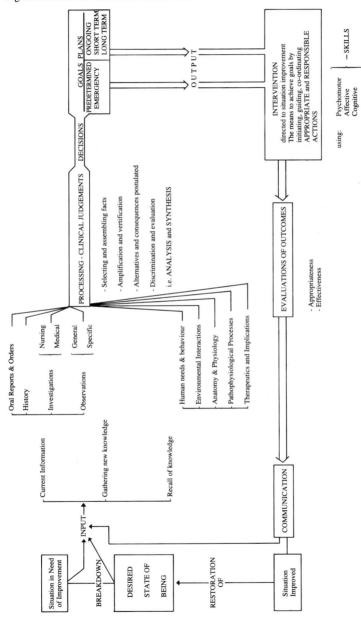

The behaviours and skills inherent in making informed judgments, of initiating and evaluating actions taken and of reflecting on patient outcomes and care systems cannot be developed vicariously; nor should they be developed by a process or osmosis, trial and error on the job after graduation.

An educational process which reflects the demands of practice such as nursing must allow the learner to develop, a sense of responsibility by being responsible; the ability to initiate and manage and evaluate wisely, by "rehearsing" these skills; the ability to engage continuously in a meaningful learning process by carrying out the learning themselves. Who does the work, does the learning whether in simulated or actual situations. Evaluation of the first course and of two cohorts of graduates has been encouraging despite the earlier limited nature of the PBL programme.

Variations in the learner-managed-learning aspect of the total curriculum

The second issue refers to variations in learner-managed aspects of a curriculum. At the University of Western Sydney, Macarthur, the course has a structure and organisation laid down in the formal curriculum document. There are a number of reasons for this not the least of which is the need to provide evidence to the professional registering body that the acquisition of knowledge, skills and competences as stipulated by that body will indeed be a feature of the programme no matter how different the approach to learning. (Relinquishing control of curriculum decisions to the degree that has occurred has meant a considerable adjustment on the part of the statutory body.) A further practice constraint in determining the degree of structure for the organisational aspects of the curriculum is the large number (800) of students involved with an intake of 300 per year into the three-year undergraduate programme. For example the limited number of clinical facilities demands a careful management scheme to allow all students to gain the full range of experiences necessary to qualify them for the single register which in turn enables them to practise as beginning practitioners in any of three different nursing fields. The law requires such experiences to be supervised by appropriated qualified faculty to ensure patient safety and effective care. Therefore the decisions about the various organisational aspects have been governed by the accountability to a registering body; the need to satisfy ethical legal requirements and to demonstrate to the public that graduates are competent; and the need to overcome considerable logistical problems.

Within these necessarily structured elements of the curriculum, the process of learning however is predominantly learner managed. Figure 8.2 identifies schematically the time frame in which those dimensions of the learning process, which are the subject of some structuring and other "directiveness", become the responsibility of the learner. As students enter the programme without prior experience in directing their own learning or in the use of the enquiry process, some structure and guidance is provided initially, decreasing rapidly.

Implementation of the learner-managed-learning process

The third of the four issues focuses on the implementation process and in particular on that aspect in which the students accept the major responsibility for learning. Students function in 'home' groups of 15-24 for campus-based learning, depending on the year, and in groups of 8 in clinical settings, with each group having one faculty member as facilitator. It is within the home group that the learning stimulus is presented. Such a stimulus has its origin in an actual patient/client situation to which students are expected to respond in their role of care giver. As happens in reality, patients conditions and circumstances change. Therefore students are presented with a series of such stimuli known as blocks which constitute a learning 'package' referred to as a situation improvement package (SIP). The duration of the exploration of one package may vary but always includes one week of related clinical experience.

A limited amount of data is provided, mostly in printed form in the classroom, though some stimulus material has been prepared as a combination of print and audio-visual; interactive video and computer packages are also being tested. Typically students will meet for two, two hour sessions and one, one hour each week (Figure 8.3). The purpose of these sessions is to respond to the data, identifying what additional information is required, what their learning needs are and ultimately to share what they have learnt, in order to prepare a situation improvement summary (SIS). They achieve this outcome by group and individual activities using enquiry and processing skills, for example during the first encounter students, when confronted with the first block of stimulus material, will respond by the:

1)   identification of facts, inferences and cues.

2)   categorisation of this data into physical, social psychological, life style and/or environmental factors.

3)   identification of situations in need of improvement

4)   which they perceive to be the main problems.

5)   generation of hypotheses about these situations.

6)   decision/s about how to test the hypotheses - often what further data they need.

(Meanwhile the facilitator allows the students to do the work but will act by clarifying and challenging student responses.)

Students have access to a resource file which may contain papers/articles, patient charts and in the case of one SIP a file of questions and responses to those questions from the patient and relatives.

Following the first group encounter, students work independently identifying and pursuing their own learning needs using a variety of resources. Sometimes students will visit outside centres or groups or individuals or simply use the library. Staff may be consulted on learning issues according to their individual expertise.

The second encounter usually lasts for one hour during which students themselves present their list of learning issues which have emerged and may then contribute what they know. It is then decided who will pursue what in more depth in order that they gain fuller understanding of the patient, his/her condition and influencing or causal factors. As a result of this preliminary activity they will be able to evaluate previously generated hypotheses and add to their cognitive structures knowledge from the various disciplines.

Fig 8.2 TIME FRAME OF THE LEARNING PROCESS

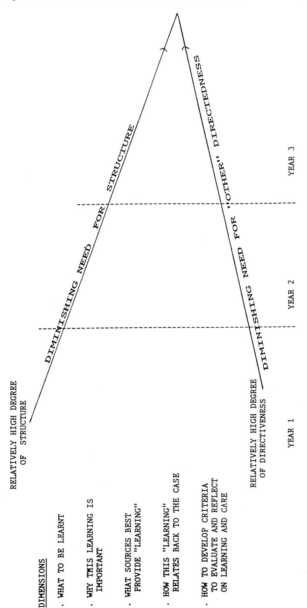

RELATIVELY HIGH DEGREE
OF STRUCTURE

DIMINISHING NEED FOR STRUCTURE

DIMINISHING NEED FOR "OTHER" DIRECTEDNESS

RELATIVELY HIGH DEGREE
OF DIRECTIVENESS

YEAR 1   YEAR 2   YEAR 3

PASSIVE TO ACTIVE LEARNER

FACILITATION : CHANGES IN DEGREE OF STRUCTURE AND DIRECTIVENESS

DIMENSIONS

· WHAT TO BE LEARNT

· WHY THIS LEARNING IS
  IMPORTANT

· WHAT SOURCES BEST
  PROVIDE "LEARNING"

· HOW THIS "LEARNING"
  RELATES BACK TO THE CASE

· HOW TO DEVELOP CRITERIA
  TO EVALUATE AND REFLECT
  ON LEARNING AND CARE

Fig 8.3 LEARNING ACTIVITIES FOR ANSIP

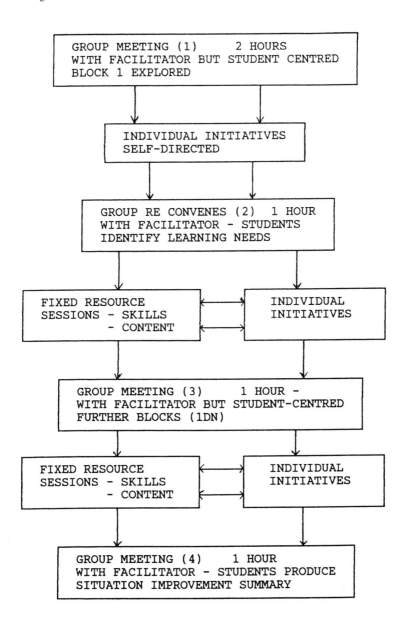

In response to the identification of certain specific learning needs fixed resource sessions may be programmed to allow the presentation of content not readily available to students. Similarly arrangements are made for the demonstration and practice of procedural skills in simulated ward settings.

In the third encounter students share what they have learnt (knowledge, skills, values) from the exploration of learning issues. The facilitator ensures accuracy of input and seeks further elaboration if necessary.

1) the students relate what has been learnt to this particular situation (facilitator may need to prompt and/or foster networking of information).

2) they evaluate their hypotheses in light of the new knowledge and decide whether to retain and pursue, reject or hold pending further amplification (facilitator may prompt to establish justifications for their decisions).

3) they then make clinical judgments for each hypothesis to be pursued.

4) they proceed to identify care activity stimuli and to prioritise them (facilitator may prompt students to cause them to relate their conclusions to our conceptual models which provide the nursing orientation).

5) they develop individually a "situation improvement summary" (SIS) that is, a care programme in accordance with their exploration of the block (facilitator provides feedback in relation to care proposed or given and about the enquiry process adopted).

This process is repeated for each block of data presented in one SIP. A situation improvement summary or series of such summaries will record the process of enquiry and the application of content to the specific care proposals. By the time the SIP is completed students also will have reflected individually on:

1) what they did and with what result;

2) whether they would do it differently next time;

3) if so, how;

4) the role of other members in their subgroups; and

5) their own self-evaluation of their overall performance using set criteria.

The value of reflection and of the self-evaluation process cannot be over estimated. Students become accustomed to using and later designing criteria against which evaluation judgments are made. Support for their decisions is provided by the students who cite incidents to justify their decisions. The ability to behave in this way has become so automatic that they are noticeably less defensive when being assessed; they require objective criteria to be applied and have influenced other staff in adopting the processes.

Evaluation of the learner-managed-learning approach

The final issue, which deals with the evidence that the approach works, deserves to be addressed in its own right. However space does not permit more than a brief summary statement. Three groups of graduates are now in the work force. Formal evaluation has taken place, initially conducted by School-based working party. In addition a comprehensive study has been undertaken by Associate Professor McMillan who has targetted a sample of 1988 graduates (n=50) and staff with whom they work (n=10). The study reports have been comprehensive and justify the following claims about graduates.

1)   they are comfortable with the idea of personal responsibility for ongoing learning;

2)   they seek additional knowledge or confirmation of their knowledge base daily;

3)   that whilst sometimes anxious they feel particularly well-equipped to cope with change;

4)   they feel that they show "initiative", are self-directed in their approach to patient care and cope well with "novel" situations; and

5)   they believe that they use a problem-solving strategy - automatically on most occasions.

Conclusion

There is no doubt that learner-managed-learning, as an educational approach, is valid in respect of the most desirable and often talked about general educational outcomes. It has been our experience that, ownership of the learning process has generated a high degree of motivation; having to explore what virtually are unknown situations and having to propose and test the solutions has resulted in increased self confidence and has developed skills and processes in learning-how-to-learn. Adopting this approach has become second nature to the majority and has been transferred to the work situation after graduation. Further, by requiring students to set their own goals, to reflect on their progress and to undertake criterion referenced self and peer assessment when they become graduates they carry over these behaviours into their everyday life and importantly into their professional practice - causing others also to evaluate existing practices.

When these characteristics/behaviours are also inherent in the professional functions and profile of graduates of a course with a learner management philosophy, then not only is the approach educationally sound but it is professionally valid.

I indicated at the outset that the degree of success achieved by implementing this practice-based programme was due to more than the self-directed aspect. For this reason it has been difficult to isolate the learner-managed elements from the total approach of a reiterative problem-based programme. Nevertheless we remain convinced that the person who does the work does the learning.

REFERENCES

Andersen B M(1976) <u>Basic nurse education curriculum</u>. A research report submitted to the Commission on Advanced Education, Sydney: Cumberland College of Health Sciences

Andersen B M(1978) <u>A basic nurse-education curriculum evaluation project incorporating an investigation into the cognitive aspects of clinical judgment</u>. Sydney: NSW College of Nursing

Diploma of Applied Science (Nursing) (1984) Macarthur Institute of Higher Education, Sydney

Diploma of Health Science (Nursing)(1989) University of Western Sydney Macarthur, Sydney

Report of the evaluation working party (August 1989) School of Nursing and Health Studies, Macarthur Institute of Higher Education, Sydney

CHAPTER 9

Reviewing Self-Managed Learning Assessment

By

Ginny Eley

Introduction

I have always been fascinated by assessment. No matter how the learning process is designed and managed, the nature of assessment casts its shadow backwards, determining what is perceived to be important, what is the essence of the course for the student, focusing staff attention towards given ends, and, for the outside world, determining the quality of the experience as measured through its outcomes.

As an essential stage of the education process, assessment needs to be congruent with its underlying philosophy and principles. Believing in learner centred education as I do, by which I understand recognising students' abilities to engage in identifying their own learning needs, choosing appropriate processes for meeting these, and establishing desired outcomes, then I also value their ability to recognise the quality of what is produced. Learner centred assessment means that the learner is essentially involved in evaluating the quality of the outcomes of the learning process.

Power in the assessment process

I see power as the central concept in analysing assessment processes. In this context, I interpret power as being whose definition of reality is recognised as being true. This leads to three broad categories.

1. Power over: the education establishment Here the teacher, the examining board, external assessors, and/or other educational professionals are perceived to be the only ones with the necessary knowledge and skill to determine and assess outcomes. While at its most evident in examinations, much experiential learning involving projects or placements still falls within this category through the reliance on the teacher marking of the work, according to general criteria determined by educationalists.

2. Power over: the student One reaction to the power of the education establishment is to assert the power of the student over the learning process. The logical conclusion of this approach is to assert that the student's definition of reality prevails. The difficulty for me in this is that the basic assumption about power remains the same: a patriarchal model of relationships as essentially conflictful, a perception of reality in which there has to be a "right" answer, and, while roles may be reversed, a continuation of "power over" structures, where the definition of one group is perceived to have higher credibility than that of the other.

When power is defined in terms of relationships where A has the ability to get B to do something which they might otherwise choose not to, then the structures we create will reflect this conflictful model, by building in asymmetrical relationships, specifying the respective power bases of the various parties, seeking to establish the legitimate authority for those whose definition should prevail. Our frameworks for making sense of the world determine the relationships we create through our actions. Therefore when our designs for assessment are based on establishing whose definitions are valid, even when we are fighting for the rights of students, we are still locked into a limited, and patriarchal, perception of power.

Other possibilities emerge once we engage with power from a different perspective. Empowering encaptures a process whereby, in relation to others, we discover our own sources of energy and creativity, leading to positive action in the world with and through others. This view of power is not zero sum, where if I have power, it is at the expense of others, but rather one in which we use our own power, while at the same time recognising the power of others. Recognising the existence of multiple realities (Lincoln & Gubba 1965) where individual perceptions of reality are all context bound, and all have validity within these contexts, then empowering is a process which recognises different perceptions, and through dialogue, works to find a common language to represent what is shared between individuals in a given context. In the learner managed learning assessment process, this can be seen as a search for a common definition for all those involved with the individual in the learning process. This leads to my third category.

3. Power together: collaborative assessment. This model of power assumes that student, peers and staff work together to secure a common view of assessment and its outcomes, based on hearing and understanding different perspectives, and seeking to secure agreement which values all perspectives. This model is essentially collaborative, dependent on reaching consensus.

This paper is based on our experience of assessment on the Postgraduate Diploma in Management by Self Managed Learning at the then Polytechnic of East London, where the underlying model of power is that of "power together". As the course is within the established educational system, there is a need for accountability in terms of its processes and its outcomes to satisfy other professionals within the system.

It is not always easy to work on an empowerment model, where we value our own power, and that of others. Participants bring to the process a model of "power over", while hearing the words about self responsibility, previous experience of education leads them to defer to the teacher as expert, looking to us for expert solutions, deferring to our opinions. Becoming aware of these models, asserting their own power, their right to define their solutions through some form of counter dependence, and eventually recognising staff as a valuable source of knowledge, skills and "history" with whom they can work productively is a process that continues throughout the course, often as an iterative process.

For staff too, it can be difficult. For some time I oscillated uncertainly between wanting to assert my own specialist knowledge and experience as more valid than that of students, and wanting to restrain my own power sources to respect their knowledge - a belief that reducing my power built up theirs. Both positions felt inauthentic, and both could be justified by what participants were asking for at various stages on the course. Being ready to acknowledge and value my own expertise, both in terms of process and specialist management knowledge, being ready to share and use this, and leave others to work with it as they will, allows me to recognise differences in role etc, and to see empowering as a process, whereby working openly I can enable other.

The Postgraduate Diploma in Management by Self Managed Learning

This postgraduate diploma is based on a self managed learning process, which means that participants review their current situations, define their development needs and objectives, design ways of achieving these, and specify the evidence they will produce, as well as criteria for assessment. These individual programmes are incorporated in contracts, which the individual negotiates with peers and staff. The assessment focuses on attainments related to the contract specification.

The course started in 1980. Part-time over 2 years, the participants have been existing managers, mainly graduates, seeking to improve their management performance. Drawn from the private, public and voluntary sectors, and from a range of positions, they have little in common apart from a readiness to take responsibility for their own learning process. Over time we have seen the proportion of women on the course increasing, so that they now form 75% of the intake.

Learning sets form the core experience of the course. Groups of 6 participants with a staff member as adviser/facilitator, and a co-adviser, usually an ex course member, meet regularly. In this set, we work together to help individual members design and carry through their individual programmes. The set also carries our assessment, with all members participating equally. Participants also link in to specialist resources within the University to provide expertise to help their learning, and specialist tutors views are also taken into account in the assessment process.

Assessment Process

Looking at the assessment process in more detail, it contains the following stages:

1) The early identification of objectives and learning outcomes by participants as part of the contracting process. These are the outcome of discussion and negotiation in the set, where the focus is on the individual as a whole person managing; each is encouraged to find a voice to explore the uniqueness of their experience, and to look to individual outcomes. External examiners receive contracts and meet with participants at this stage.

2) The monitoring of the implementation of the programmes, when in the set, members account for how programmes are being realised in practice, bringing evidence of what they are doing. We are collectively developing an understanding of the

relationship between the words of the contract and their realisation in actuality; a common language is developing.

3)   Reviewing and revision of the contract in the light of experience. The contract provides members with a tool to analyse and understand their managing and learning processes. With this understanding they are able to write more explicit and realistic contracts, with outcomes specified in a language which other members share, and embedded in a shared context.

4)   Developing an assessment process. The course regulations stipulate that assessment takes place within the set, on the basis of individual contracts, and with the input of the views of a second staff member (to conform to University regulations). At the beginning of the second year members are asked to specify how this assessment will take place, and how it will be accessible to external examiners. This involves surfacing assumptions about standards, negotiating these, as well as devising in advance processes to reconcile differences. This process is then negotiated with external examiners.

5)   Carrying out individual assessments. Each set then assesses individuals according to their agreed procedures. From my experience, while each set has a distinctive process, there are similarities, in that most will spread the assessment of individual contract products over a period of time, culminating in an overall assessment, when fulfilment of the contract as a whole is looked at, allowing for recognition of other learning over the course, and taking account of areas which are linked to more than one area of work.

6)   Access of externals to the assessment process. We perceive the role of externals to involve monitoring that assessment is carried out according to agreed procedures, in a non collusive way.

In our ten years of experience we have found no need to change the broad framework of the assessment process. Within this, there has been considerable variation in how sets have operated. This variation, resulting from the discussions within sets when members have shared assumptions, surfaced the deep emotions stirred by assessment, and explored ways both of respecting individual contracts and maintaining the standard implied by the notion of postgraduateness, has enabled us as staff to explore the process, and to examine the power issues raised by the different roles.

Reviewing the Experience

Standards: What does POSTGRADUATENESS mean?

If we are to engage together on making assessments about the award of a postgraduate diploma, we need a collective view about that this standard means in this context. This discussion is stimulated by the need to produce an assessment process for external examiners early in the second year.

It is not easy! Sets can spend considerable time on this but the benefits show when we have a mutually agreed statement to help us cope with differences experienced when assessing work. At this stage we start by uncovering the unconscious notions of postgraduateness which members bring, usually reflecting the production of a number of "academic" papers. Fears about assessment from previous experience are shared; anger at what has frequently been experienced as inhuman, labelling, unfair, devaluing one's own judgement and leaving one powerless. From this we start to build; looking at what each wanted to achieve from the course; looking for what would be "good enough" in a general sense. This is search for a holistic definition of postgraduateness which honours the spirit of individual contracts, and values all aspects of their development as managers. While traditional elements of theory remain, communication becomes more widely interpreted to embrace forms suitable for the intention of different elements. Change and development are often incorporated, as is action in the world. Sometimes the set adopts a general statement covering all members, in others each member incorporates their own version in their contracts. These statements are then shared with our external examiners.

We are sometimes asked to provide models of what others have done, or alternatively, as staff, to tell the set how to do it. While either course would undoubtedly save time, and make things easier, we believe it is important to stay with the process of establishing for ourselves what are appropriate definitions for the contracts of this particular set. Sharing, testing out what words mean, testing statements against individuals intentions, gradually taking ownership of that is emerging is an important part of the process of empowering, so that all not only know what they are going to produce, but are clear about criteria for its assessment and have a language to engage with the rest of the set.

Roles.

It is all very well, you may be asking, but this paints a rather idealistic picture of collaborative assessment, passing over what must be different roles for those engaged in the process. What follows is my personal experience of how roles vary in the assessment process.

First of all the individual being assessed is responsible for "managing" their assessment; that is producing work, ensuring that the set has the evidence it requires, timing assessments to fit meeting patterns, and so on. They also take responsibility for presenting their work, and making explicit the extent to which it meets their objectives and set criteria, and for supplying additional information that other members may require to reach a conclusion. Each individual also needs to reach a pass/fail judgement on their own work.

Peers in the set engage first by giving monitoring help in the course of the programme. At assessment, they have digested the information provided, and share their judgements of what is produced, using the agreed criteria, asking for clarification if necessary. This provides a mirror back to the individual, and puts their self evaluation in the context of that of others. A rich picture is developing. Often set members disagree on certain aspects; through discussion we are usually able to either supply additional information, clarify meanings, or investigate further where this comes from in the context of whole programmes, and so resolve difficulties.

As a **staff set adviser** I have a special role from my knowledge of the stated procedures and as a history carrier, which I share with the set. I have a broad awareness of how long different processes will take, and so I have responsibility for placing the management of assessment in general on the set agenda. I also have an awareness of how standards are interpreted elsewhere on the Diploma and in the academic world, I contribute this to the set as part of the process of building an assessment process, to the best of my ability as information to be used as appropriate. My experience suggests that when this comes in the process of discussion, rather than at the beginning, then the set is better able to use my contributions to inform rather than to dictate their deliberations. In actual assessments my opinion is received as other set members, and I find is usually in tune with what others are saying. As the set is required to reach consensus, so my assessment both carries no more weight than that of the others and cannot be ignored.

A **second assessor**, normally a specialist tutor, is required to participate in the assessment process, by putting views on what has been produced from outside the set. These views are seen as important, but are again not vetos; the set takes these views as information to help reach a final conclusion. I have seen specialist tutor views supporting a pass when a set has decided that the work was not yet passing - in the narrow academic frame definition of postgraduate it was inadequate.

The **external examiner** ensures that assessment processes are appropriate, and applied non collusively. Through early reading of contracts and meetings with course participants they are in a position to alert members to contracts which may be inappropriate, and so put information into the system. We have been fortunate in having externals who understood the course, have helped us expand our understanding of the processes involved, and carry academic credibility in the world outside.

While they do not generally directly assess participants work, they have detailed access to the set assessment processes. One early external happily (?) listened to hours of tape recording of set meetings. The external examiners provide a safety net, a means of reaching a decision if sets cannot reach a decision, in 10 years they have only twice been called on to fulfil this role.

Coping with Difference

While the course process develops understanding and a common language, and provides monitoring feedback, almost inevitably difficulties do arise. The judgement element of assessment means that differences are revealed, and their consequences worked through. (One of the first difficulties that we often face is that created by the inclusion of a judgemental role for members whose previous mode was facilitative/supportive.)

As members become clearer about themselves as managers, about their underlying values, and better able to analyse the management processes prevailing in their organisations, so they use this learning as a perspective on fellow set members. Because of the importance of the set in the learning process, aspects of this might be valid, and built into the criteria. But this is not always so. Members may not share political values, and these may affect priorities as managers, and the solutions offered to management problems, as in the case where a manager in a conservative local authority used contracting out services as a study, which another member found ideologically impossible. A difficult process of recognising the different value bases ensued, valuing the other in spite of disagreeing fundamentally over what was important, and seeing how individual and set criteria applied to what had been produced enabled us to reach consensus. It remained uncomfortable, but enabled all to voice how fundamental values affected judgement of individual performance.

The other major issue which emerges is between the letter and the spirit of the assessment documentation. What is written emerges from hours of deliberation in the set. Because of this understanding of the ground of the language, it would be a travesty of the process to treat the language as isolated from the process from which it emerged. The assessment process both uses the language of the formal written agreement, and interprets this through the collective knowledge of the set process. This is true for both the set assessment process document, and for individual contracts. It is not unusual for set members who want to pass to argue for one interpretation, while others remind them of what was said at the time of contract negotiation. The on going memory of the set enables us to engage with the letter and the spirit of our agreed procedures.

The assessment process is often lengthy. It can occupy one third of the course, although in other ways it can be said to begin from the very first day. But because the assessment process is an integral part of the learning process, it is in many ways the perfect vehicle for helping managers learn, with its emphasis not only on managing ones own learning, but taking responsibility for the quality of the outcomes of that learning, and finding ways of engaging with others in finding a common language to mirror achievements and attainments. It is the most rigorous and demanding assessment I have come across; and according to our course participants, the most rewarding, and the most growth producing.

REFERENCES

Lincoln S Y & Gubba E O(1985) <u>Naturalistic Inquiry</u> Sage

ASSESSING LEARNER-MANAGED-LEARNING; PROBLEMS OF PROCESS AND PRODUCT; A CASE STUDY OF THE UNIVERSITY OF EAST LONDON

By

NORMAN GRAVES

Introduction

There is a sense in which all learning has to be managed by the learner. The learning of something by someone can never take place without the learner being directly involved. One need only consider the learning of a physical or manipulative skill to understand that while a teacher can demonstrate the skill, encourage and guide the learner, he or she can never directly cause the individual to learn; only the student can do the learning. It is true that in some cases, for example in the learning of attitudes; the learner may not be conscious of what has been learnt, but nevertheless, attitudes are not "caught" without the learner being a participant in the process.Where "brainwashing" has occurred then we are up against what is a conceptual problem since such an activity cannot easily fall within the definition of education.

My understanding of learner-managed-learning is that this refers to a process where the latitude offered to the learner is greater than is usual in formal education.This latitude is given by allowing the student a wide choice in deciding what he or she will learn, and in allowing him or her to decide how he or she will learn, that is by giving the student a choice of the means by which he or she will acquire the knowledge, skills and attitudes he or she has decided to learn.Strictly, it would be better to call such schemes "independent study", since learner-managed-learning can apply to a wide range of courses.The problem which inevitably arises, is how can such learning be assessed, granted that society requires some assurance that the teaching received has not been in vain? It is with the issue of assessing this kind of learner-managed-learning that this chapter will be concerned.

Personal involvement

My own qualifications for dealing with such a topic are limited,as my involvement with the assessment of independent study in higher education dates from the summer of 1990 and like many things in life, it occurred partly by accident. The Polytechnic of East London has been running since 1976, a third year higher education course leading to a degree(BA/BSc) by independent study.Independent Study at the Polytechnic in effect means that a student can, within limits, choose what he or she wishes to study granted this is judged to be at a level appropriate to higher education. In the United Kingdom it is the practice of all higher education institutions to appoint "external examiners" who sample the work produced by students which has already been assessed by their own tutors. The "external examiners" are so called because they come from other institutions(other polytechnics or universities) than those whose students are being examined. The functions of an external examiner are to ensure that the students are fairly treated and to act as guarantors of the standard of the qualification being issued, that is to indicate that the degree of one university or polytechnic is equivalent in level to that given by others. This is an exercise in human judgement rather than a mathematically accurate process, but with experienced examiners in particular disciplines, it works reasonably well, since these have experiential knowledge of what standards are acceptable in higher education in their own subject areas.

Thus when at short notice the Polytechnic of East London asked me to undertake the role of Chief External Examiner for the degree in Independent Study, I was faced with what was to me a new situation. Whilst I had plenty of experience as an "external examiner", this had always been in the context of a particular subject area(geography) or in the field of teacher education. My problem was to come to grips with the role of being a guarantor of standards for a degree which was not concerned with a specific discipline or even with a range of like minded disciplines such as medicine.

The nature of independent study at the Polytechnic (now University) of East London

It is important to be aware of the nature of the course whose product is being assessed. By `product' I mean the knowledge, skills and attitudes acquired by particular students at the end of a three year course,as manifested by the course work they produced.

I will not dwell on the intricacies of the many routes whereby a student may arrive at the threshold of the third year, but it is necessary to know that such students will not have followed similar courses in previous years.Consequently these students will not be equipped with a similar set of skills and will not possess the same knowledge either qualitatively or quantitatively.However, it is expected that all students enrolling on a course of independent study:

1)   "are willing to take responsibility for planning and managing their own learning"

2)   "have specific interest not fully catered for by taught courses".

A student embarking on a third and final year degree course needs first to draft a proposal for a plan of study which is negotiated with a tutor from the Independent Study Coordinating Unit and with a tutor who is a specialist in the area of the proposed study. This proposal has to indicate:

1)   in what way the student is qualified to undertake such study

2)   what the proposed study is about

3)   the time scale over which the study is to be undertaken

4)   the resources needed for the study

5)   the justification for the programme

6)   how the work produced is to be assessed.

The whole proposal, once negotiated with the tutors concerned is placed before a "Registration and Assessment Board" which needs to be satisfied that the programme of study is feasible, educationally sound and could not have been undertaken by following a standard taught course.

In general, the work submitted for assessment consists of:

1)   Course Work - usually two or more essays of about 5000 words each (not more than 60% of total marks)

2)   A Dissertation - about 10 000 words(40-60% of total marks)

3)   A Critical Review - the student's own evaluation of the programme he or she has undertaken(10-20% of total marks).

I will give a few examples to clarify the way in which the assessed work is structured and to indicate the kind of topics chosen by students. One student in the 1991 cohort studied the historical evidence for the persecution of Jews in Europe. Thus his two course work essays examined Jewish Pogroms in 19th century Russia and the Dreyfus case in France; his dissertation was on the nature of 19th century Jewish immigration into the East End of London with special reference to the attempts made to provide schooling for immigrant children. Another student made a study of the relationships between the African National Congress, the Trade Unions and the Inkatha Movement in Natal within the context of contemporary events in the Republic of South Africa. Yet another student studied the way in which pollution in the United Kingdom was being monitored, given the official(legal) definition of pollution then extant.

Thus in all cases the structure of the products to be assessed is similar but the content of each product is very different. Therefore in considering the assessment of the products of independent study, it is necessary to be clear about precisely what principles are incorporated into independent study. These are given in a document produced by the Polytechnic in April 1991 entitled UNDERGRADUATE PROGRAMMES BY INDEPENDENT STUDY. The following contains the essence of those principles.

Independent Study is a learning process which promotes both specific and general capabilities in students by giving them the opportunity, as individuals and as members of learning groups, to be responsible for:

1)   The formulation of the problem or challenge of their own higher education.(They have to decide what they want from higher education);

2)   The planning of a programme of study in response to that challenge;

3)   The negotiation of that programme within the academic

	context of the polytechnic;
4)	Engaging in debate about criteria relevant to the judgement of successful performance;
5)	The submission of plans of their proposed programme for approval after internal and external scrutiny;
6)	Effectively collaborating with others;
7)	The completion of their studies with assistance and not direction from others;
8)	Critical reflection upon and critical dialogue about their progress in learning;
9)	The submission of their own distinctive work for external scrutiny as evidence of their achievement;
10)	Critically reviewing the overall effectiveness of their programmes of study.
11)	These responsibilities of the student define the sense in which independent study may be considered learner-centered self directed and negotiated learning.

What is being assessed?

There is little doubt in my mind that this statement about the principles of independent study(or of learner-managed-learning) emphasizes the process followed by the learner rather than the content of what he/she is learning. I use the word content here to mean the knowledge(ie the concepts and principles),the skills and attitudes which may be learned. Yet the assessment which is being undertaken is an assessment of what the student has produced in concrete terms and relates closely to the area of knowledge which he/she has investigated. If I may return briefly to the case of the student who had studied Jewish persecution in the 19th century, he was working in the area of history, religion and sociology. It might be argued that the work he produced could be judged on the accuracy of his historical knowledge and reasoning, on his understanding of various jewish religious concepts and of the interaction between Jewish immigrant cultures and indigenous cultures. How he came to acquire this knowledge and understanding might be seen as irrelevant to the issue of assessing his products.

I understand, of course, that the proponents of independent study and learner-managed-learning will testify that the quality of the product will be much influenced by the process through which the learner has passed in order to compose the product. There little doubt, they will aver, that process and product are not independent of one another, and that in general, the more intellectually stimulating the process through which a student is guided to learn something, then the greater the benefit in terms of the knowledge and skills the student has acquired can use. I would find little to quarrel with in such a proposition.But I would argue that since the emphasis of independent study is on process of learning then the assessment should at least recognize this by giving greater weight to this aspect of total learning.

If this argument is correct, then how can a dual assessment of both process and product takes place?

ASSESSING PROCESS AND PRODUCT

It seems to me that, given the structure of assessment at present in operation for independent study at the University of East London, some means can be found of allocating credit for the stages through which the student manages his/her own learning. In the case of the third year course for a degree by independent study, this could be done by allocating marks in the following manner:

> 10% for the formulation of the problem or challenge which starts the whole process
>
> 20% for the submission of a plan of study
>
> 20% for course work
>
> 30% for the dissertation
>
> 20% for the critical review

This would effectively give 50% of total marks to the process aspect of learning since I regard the Critical Review as a reflection on the process of learning which has occurred during the year.If this were accepted, then both process and product would be equally assessed.

It may be objected that in the early stages of formulating a programme of study, students may not show themselves in a good light,but this would apply to all students and would therefore be fair. It may also be true that the nature of the programme of study may be a measure of the close collaboration between tutor and student, though strictly,a programme largely determined by the tutor would be a negation of independent study, and a student requiring such close guidance should be counselled against undergoing such a course.

Learner-managed-learning assessment: residual problems

What I have argued so far is that since learner-managed-learning emphasizes the process of learning, then logically some credit should be explicitly given to the way the student has operated that process. There are other issues which face anyone attempting to assess independent study, and these concern the content of the programme as revealed by the product produced by the student.The first issue concerns breadth versus depth of study. Whilst it is generally true that following a course in higher education enables a student to explore a particular subject area in depth, this is also associated with scanning the breadth of a field of study. For example, someone undertaking to study for a degree in economics may choose to concentrate on banking and monetary policy as a special interest area; but he or she will also obtain an overview of the whole field of economics: micro- and macro-economics, international trade, public finance and so on. The same would be true of someone following a course in law or biological sciences.

My experience of reading the products of independent study is that many students tend to concentrate on a very narrow area of study much more akin to what a post graduate student might do when writing a dissertation or thesis on a particular problem or issue. The problem facing an assessor of such work is that though the student may have honestly undertaken the work he or she set out to do, it is clear that background knowledge and understanding possessed by the student may be too limited to do justice to the specialist topic studied. To return to the examples given earlier, I find it difficult to accept that someone who concentrates at first degree level on Jewish persecution in 19th century Europe or on the relationship between the African National Congress, trade unions and Inkatha in Natal, has a wide enough view of the historical, economic and social context to enable him to make a balanced judgment about the events he is researching. Further if one thinks in terms of the professional outlets for such graduates, it is difficult to see how such narrow areas of study can benefit them on the job market. Whilst it is true that some students may have undertaken study in breadth in previous years, this was not evident in the work which I read. It will be argued by proponents of independent study that what matters are the intellectual skills acquired by the students rather than the substantive knowledge they have gained. Yet I have strong doubts that these two aspects of learning can be separated. Intellectual skills are varied and relate closely to the kind of disciplinary framework one is using to tackle a problem

A mathematical problem does not require the same skills as literary analysis and whilst all real life problems require more than one disciplinary framework to solve them, the researcher needs to know which frameworks are relevant in any given context.This kind of knowledge can only be gained by students if they have acquired a sufficiently wide range of substantive knowledge.

A second but related issue is the extent to which some students tend to concentrate on topics on which they have strong views; in other words they begin their study with a strong commitment to something or some organization. For example, the student who devoted his third year work to the political situation in Natal, seemed to be strongly committed to the African National Congress(ANC) and against Inkatha. Now whilst I can accept that any student may start off with very strong views of this sort, I would have expected such a student to gather evidence from both sides to explain how Inkatha and the ANC came to have strong followings, even if the end he came to the conclusion that those following Inkatha were misguided. However, the process he went through was one of gathering evidence to bolster his original pre-conception. The problem for an assessor is to decide how far the product of such independent study is flawed because the student is bigoted in his views and incapable of seeing the other side of a case, or because he was allowed to undertake such a narrow study in the first place.

Thus problems of assessing such cases have a tendency to force one back to some of the premisses of independent study which perhaps give excessive latitude to the student in allowing him or her to study too narrow a field at first degree level. It also throws a great deal of responsibility on the tutor in opening up the mind of a student whose commitment to a cause may blind him to the evidence which in a more traditional course may be put before him or her by various lecturers.

Conclusion

Independent study is an opportunity for some students who, for one reason or another find that existing taught courses do not suit their purpose. This may be because the student wishes to focus on an area not well covered by taught courses and/or because the student wishes to study in a manner which suits him or her best and does not wish to be bound by existing teaching arrangements.

Assessing such independent study where emphasis is placed on the process of learning, should in logic, involve that process as well as the product. This should not present many difficulties, as has been indicated earlier. Further the product may be assessed so as to give due weight to the processes used to achieve its completion. One institution has used the following criteria to this end:

1)   Imagination/originality

2)   Understanding and competence

3)   Critical judgement

4)   Communications skills

5)   Synthesising capacity and ability to relate to practice

6)   Broad cognitive perspective.

Assessing the product using such criteria is fair but only if the student has been warned against the dangers of excessive narrowness in the scope of his or her study. This has implications for the criteria used for the registration of programmes of study.

None of this detracts from the desirability of encouraging all students in all fields of study from managing their own learning!

SECTION B:
THEORETICAL ISSUES
AND
PRACTICAL IMPLICATIONS

CHAPTER 11

Learner-Managed-Learning:
A Metaphor for Educational Revolution?

By

Len Cairns

Introduction

Let me begin with the mandatory self-indulgent story.

Some years ago, whilst I was a Visiting Professor in Educational Psychology at the University of Arizona in the USA, I wrote the first draft of a paper on Piaget, the Swiss Developmental Psychologist. The paper was an attempt to pursue the `person' and to enlighten myself and the reader as to the personal style of Piaget by tracing views of the man, rather than his work, through his writings about himself and those of others who know him well. I wrote the paper initially also as a reaction to the concept that a colleague of the time was teaching in her course on developmental theories. The concept was the importance of the `Zeitgeist', or the `spirit of the times' as a form of cognitive organiser for an understanding of a theorist and his theory. (She used Freud, Skinner and Piaget as the basic trio of theorists for this course, which was well taught and very successful.) My problem was that the more I read and the more "detective work" I did on Piaget, the more I became convinced (some colleagues felt that I was obsessed) that Piaget was a deliberate `recluse' from the Zeitgeist around him. I wrote so and spent a good couple of pages in the first draft of the paper expounding on the manner in which I felt the Zeitgeist concept as a tool for analysis and understanding of the man, Piaget, was not appropriate. After some critical feedback from some Australian and New Zealand Educational Psychologists who basically thought that my paper was disrespectful of the great polymath, I put it aside and worked on other writing. About two years ago I came across the draft in my files, re-read it and re-wrote the paper with the attack on the Zeitgeist concept omitted. I toyed with a new title which played with the words Polymath and Polymyth to emphasise my theses that Piaget was quite deliberate in the creation of his Polymath status and that he also went to pains to keep his `persona' away from his works and his adoring audience (akin to creating himself as a Polymyth).

The revised manuscript, with a less provocative title, was sent to a respectable academic journal for consideration for publication. The referee's, all I assume historians, had a field day with my paper! The two anonymous academics rejected the paper on the grounds that it did not follow proper methods of historiography and make clear the place of the man within the socio-cultural and historical spirit of his times. Their rejection of the paper and particularly its methodology was strong and unambiguous. It appears that if one tries to ignore the `spirit of the times'; it is not without peril.

The paper remains in my file unpublished.

Background influences

I have begun this paper with this story, a little longer than it perhaps should be, as a brief introduction, to allow me to raise some points about the way my paper on Learner-Managed-Learning sits within the field and the methodology.

I am of the belief, as my title suggests, that we were, in 1991, at the peak of a pyramid of influences that herald quite an educational revolution. I state this not as a Marxist influenced educator, for I am not, nor as an Alternative educator, nor a `progressive', but rather as one who has been influenced in my educational `youth' by writers such as Rousseau, Dewey, Holt, Illich, and Neill, by discussions with speakers such as Hemmings, Henderson, Weaver, Shah, and a large number of the `World Educational Fellowship' advocates over the past 25 years and by the more recent work of Stephenson, Weil and McGill, Kolb, Boud and others in the field of Independent Learning, Experiential Learning and so on. I have also spent the last 6 years working in the development of a range of courses in the Open or Distance Education mode which has opened up a broad range of questions and offered some answers. I have found, in these separate areas, a series of parallel trends and developments that, for me, have moved from parallel towards a convergence. It is that convergence that I wish to.

An educational revolution?

I want to argue that there are a large number of different, yet related, developments in our educational and other life influences that have arisen at the same time in the 1980's and will, I believe, peak in the 1990's to offer a revolutionary approach to education in the next century which is not far away. I also believe that the Learner-Managed-Learning metaphor is now a very useful rubric around which we can analyse this revolution.

I offer this view with some trepidation as I am aware that many, many others have tried to declare that the "time is right" (or even "ripe") for educational reform, change, revolution, re-emergence or whatever other terminology they chose to use at the time. Usually, these critics have all been faced with a similar result; the "system" has continued and they have been consigned as topics in the History of Educational Ideas courses at many Universities.

I am also mindful of the admonition of Sir John Adams who wrote in the introduction to his 1922 volume on <u>Modern Developments in Educational Practice</u>, that:

> It seems inherent in human beings to regard their own period
> as one of notable change. We are continually telling each
> other that this is a critical time, that we are at the parting of
> the ways, that vital issues lie in our hands at the present
> moment. (p.2)

My view today is however, that it is not merely a time to declare or attempt to posit a "revolutionary change" but rather, I am drawing together, I believe, a set of events and describing a set of trends that have already emerged, have gathered momentum and are symptomatic of the "spirit of our times". Whilst the world reels to economic and political slumps and chaos, there are optimistic signs that some of the current developments and changes are leading to a major new order. I speak then as an observer, who may have just noticed some of the forest made up by all those trees! If some of you are clearer "forest watchers" than I, than I apologise in advance for what may seem to you today as a statement of the obvious.

Nature of the convergence

I want to propose that there are at least four major aspects on "fields" of current development related to education which are converging in some of their pathways. These four are:

1)   The Alternative educational structures and programmes movement.

2)   The Distance and Open education area.

3)   The Educational Technology field.

4)   The increasing emphasis on the importance of personal experience in life and work training and its recognition.

Let us take each of these briefly as I sketch them in some details with a broad brush.

1.   The Alternative educational structures and programmes movement.

It is interesting that the "progressivism" movements of this century appear to come in cycles and that since the mid seventies we have witnessed an apparent decline in the interest, writings and popularisation of the alternative school movement and the cries to provide "free schools" or "progressive schools" for young children. It is as though the early seventies saw this move peak for primary or elementary aged children and their schools, this being followed in the mid seventies with the alternative secondary schooling press. In the eighties we have seen some, limited, expansion and argument in the tertiary sector as a response to the forward movement of the alternative "wave" that began with the younger children in the seventies. It is as if not only did the children pass through this sequence with the wave dropping to a ripple but the educators aged and moved on to different levels, some losing their alternative fervour and others being blunted by the "system". Another view might well be that the fervour and criticism actually had some effects and the need for continuation of the level of effort thereby declined. The movements to set up alternative universities however do not appear to have been profound as yet and the most successful efforts to diverge from the older more traditional pathways for tertiary education have been via either new formal structures such as the Open University in the UK or within existing structures such as the School for Independent Learning at the East London Polytechnic (now the University of East London).

Nevertheless, whilst the developments in this area or field have been slow, and less spectacular than some of the efforts at the school level in the 1970's, there has been progress. One could argue that in many of the educational systems of the western world the "mainstream" patterns of organisational structures and curriculum have frequently adapted to many of the criticisms of the past twenty years and have become much "freer" than many educators of the 1960's would have believed possible. An obvious example that comes to mind in the "Open Classroom" movement of the late 1960's and early 1970's which spread rapidly across the

USA, Australia, New Zealand and Canada and is now, to a considerable extent, a regular feature of many school systems within those countries to the point that many young teachers have difficulty seeing the ideas as in any way "revolutionary" for their time. Many of the concepts have become a part of the normal system.

The advent of the Open University in the UK has also expanded the tertiary educational offerings and opportunities in a way that even the originators would have been unable to foresee.

I am arguing that this trend for the development of what we previously argued for as alternative approaches and structures has become quite pervasive and many of our formal systems and structures for educational delivery and curriculum have adapted, become more flexible and are more open to change than we envisaged. I recognise that this aspect could be the subject of a major debate and that not everyone will agree with my view of the scene!

2.   The Distance and Open Education area.

There have been great strides forward in the field now known as Distance Education. What used to be, some twenty years ago, "correspondence education" or "external studies", which was perceived by many as a cheap, less than valid but expedient process of delivery of courses at the post-secondary level of education has become a burgeoning field of educational enterprise as well as academic study. There are a number of definitional debates still raging within the Distance Education field but it is safe to say that in the past most definitions dealt with the topic in terms of the provision of learning/teaching materials for a set course (mostly by way of printed materials) and the attempt to provide some teaching or tutorial assistance for the learner/student. Inherent in many of the earlier conceptualisations was a belief that there was a definite need to agonise over the provision of interaction with the teacher and fellow students as a form of compensation for the tyranny of distance and isolation the learners must surely feel and with which they have to deal. We now know that many students prefer to study quite independently or at least to have some options. Current developments in this field are swinging towards what is now frequently described as more "Open" education. Rumble (1989) has argued in the journal titled "Open Learning", that the terms "Distance Learning" and "Open Learning" have been misused in the past few years and that a distinction needs to be drawn between the two. Rumble's position is clear; "Open learning" should refer to the nature of the education offered to students whereas "Distance Learning" refers to a method of education. Others in the field have debated this aspect with Rumble (Lewis, 1990) and the issue has led to a good deal of consideration as to the nature, patterns and purposes of education that does not require the learner and the teacher to be present contiguously at some campus centre. I will argue later that this realisation, that this issue is an emergent, important consideration about education in general, is one of the most significant issues for us to address in the near future.

3.   The Educational Technology field.

Like no other aspect of life in this century, the emergence of modern technology has exploded many of the previously held beliefs about knowledge, teaching, learning, transmission of information and communication. That we can send a human to the moon has been amazing enough, but that we sat at home and watched this momentous event unfold on our TV screens is truly incredible. Early in 1991 we sat, all over the world, at home and watched a war develop, erupt and finish, almost as if it were some grand opera! We have begun to reach sights and experiences via modern technology which makes it increasingly difficult to determine fact from fantasy.

It is now technologically possible to live and work (depending on your vocation of course) almost anywhere provided you have access to the appropriate technology, power and telephone lines. The storage and transmission of information, images, movement, colour, sound and interactive possibilities with all of these elements is now a reality rather than a dream. Most of the rapid advances in this area have come in the last twenty years at an increasingly accelerated rate. One may wonder what mass available tools and devices might emerge in the few years to the year 2000.

The implications of such technology for the structure, curriculum and delivery of what we now call education are as broad as the limits of ingenuity of those seeking to use it. With the advent of mass production and home distribution of many of these devices around the world, it is obvious that the type of learner demand on the educational industry will shift significantly towards more home-based, learner selected and controlled activities.

4.   The increasing emphasis on the importance of personal experience in life and work training and its recognition.

Writing in 1976, John Holt opened his book *Instead of Education* with the following statement:

> This is a book in favour of doing - self-directed, purposeful,
> meaningful life and work - and against `education' - learning
> cut off from active life and done under pressure of bribe or
> threat, greed and fear. (p.7)

This volume was probably one of Holt's least popular, though it was fairly widely read at the time. It is interesting that the current resurgence of movements towards experiential learning, recognition of life experiences and the coming together of informal and more formal educational enterprises with recognition of work and life training experiences towards the more formal awards could be seen as embodying some of Holt's cries in that volume. As with the "Open" education concept, there is now a much greater recognition that learners do not necessarily achieve success in linear, step-wise models and that entry "hurdles" to formal training and educational opportunities are most likely economic and politically based concepts with little or no educational basis. Of course, there are powerful elements of all societies who still argue, and most successfully, for "basics" and "standards" which generally mean exclusivitiy and restrictive practices and opportunities. The growth in many countries of more open entry and differentially paced programmes which are in high demand and expanding in participation is clear evidence that there is an increasing awareness and expectation of the rights of all citizens to access and experience personal development activities of their choice and pattern. Changes in the life styles and work patterns of families and across the former gender-based biases has meant that the demands made of traditional educational providers has to lead to major change and re-organisation. That this may occur in a short period is seen by some as a revolutionary effect.

Contiguous with the developments in these four key areas has been the rapid increase in the rise of consideration for models or approaches to learning and education which can be characterised as those which emphasise *the changing locus or control in learning.*

What these various approaches have in common is that they all emphasise the learner as a prime "mover and shaker" or as the key force in the process, rather than the teacher.

Common theoretical perspectives

Some of these approaches share much in common theoretical ground and personnel, while others appear to have blossomed within entirely separate disciplines and subjects.

The approaches as they have been identified by various authors and groups include:

> Experiential Learning (Keeton (1976, (Kolb (1984), Weil and McGill (1989)).
>
> Self Directed Learning (Knowles (1975), Hammond and Collins (1991)).
>
> Independent Learning (Dressel and Thompson (1973), Boud (1981, 1988), Henderson and Natheson (1984)).
>
> Action Learning (Revens (1980)).
>
> Reflective Learning (Schon, (1987)).
>
> Open Learning (Paine (1988), Lewis and Spencer (1986), Rumble (1989)).
>
> Student Controlled Learning (Stephenson (1987)).

There is no space to elaborate each of these different yet related concepts and approaches. At this stage, for the sake of brevity, I would like to argue that there are identifiable similarities among these various terms and the practices and beliefs which they describe. I plan to present an expanded version of this thesis at a later stage, but for the purposes of this paper I seek your indulgence to accept the basic premises of "similarity" and "complementarity" of these variously advocated approaches.

Most emphasise that the adult student or the learner (whether he/she be a manager, a health worker or whatever) is at the centre of the approach. Some draw more on experiences whilst other approaches seek to empower the learners to take some planning control, whilst others offer students freer choices related to curriculum, pacing of learning, level of assessment and to some extent, location of study. Most emphasise learning by "doing" or a more active involvement of the learner than in traditionally taught programmes where the learner is more passive.

What then is my purpose in highlighting these similarities?

Clearly, there are, in each of these areas, sets of researchers, groups of writers and advocates and a wealth of evidence on approaches that emphasise the central role of the learner/student, be it in business or management (Revans' "Action Learning"), or Medical Education (Hammond and Collins' "Self-Directed learning") or a whole range of Tertiary level courses (Stephenson's "Student Controlled Learning"). Each of these approaches have begun to converge and overlap in theory and ideas though often the advocates of one are not often overtly aware of the other.

Learner-managed-learning: the essence of new education?

This convergence, when seen together with the previously mentioned developments in a number of educational fields of study indicates to me that there is a Zeitgeist or current spirit which is emerging that clearly emphasises the potential revolutionary change in the formal educational enterprises, particularly in adult, tertiary education from the more formal, capital intensive, campus based, contiguous course instruction structures towards less formal learner negotiated, controlled, home or work-based and self-paced approaches.

The consequences of this development are that many of our cherished and institutionalised beliefs about "ivy league" and other hallowed halls of learning will change as they become obsolete edifices of historical fascination. Some may still be sought after as places of learning and scholarship but a majority will become centres or institutions for other activities or aspects of the educational enterprise. I would contend that for many students of the future, learning will be managed and directed by them, the consumers, much more than today and that this will become the norm rather than the exception.

I wish to argue that the use of the term Learner-Managed-Learning is an appropriate metaphor and that this term is a logical and useful symbol of the convergence of much of the theory and advocacy we have been discussing.

Over the past decade the American researcher and Educational Psychologist David Berliner has been arguing that the basic (or as he calls it the "root") metaphor for the role of the teacher should be shifted from "care giver" to "manager". Berliner argues that teachers are executives who manage the key elements of resources, people and time, making hundreds of important decisions about these aspects each day they work. This is a valuable idea which is worthy of serious consideration. Not many senior managers in business and industry actually make as many key decisions in a day as does a classroom teacher. Each of the teacher's decisions may not involve large capital or be as pervasive in effects across a wide spectrum of society but to the participants they may be equally as significant as the industrial manager's decision is within his/her context at the time.

My point is that if the "manager" metaphor is accepted as the root metaphor for the teacher then an approach which shifts the locus of control about learning from the teacher to the learner should be effectively and accurately describable as "Learner Managed Learning".

Further, that this metaphor in its effects is powerful and potentially revolutionary in the educational systems we now know and experience has been presented as the logical extension and outcome of the observed convergence of the various forces and factors discussed.

REFERENCES

ADAMS John(1922) <u>Modern Developments in Education Practice</u> University of London Press

BARKER B O, FRISBIE A G and PATRICK K R(1989) Broadening the Definition of Distance Education in Light of the New Telecommunications Technologies , The American Journal of Distance Education, 3(1) 20-29.

BOUD D (Ed)(1988) Developing Student Autonomy in Learning, Kogan Page

CARL D R(1989) Media and Adult Learning: A Forum. A Response to Greville Rumble's "On Defining Distance Education" The American Journal of Distance Education 3(3) 65-67

DEWEY J(1916) Democracy and Education The Macmillan Company

DRESSEL P L and THOMPSON M M(1973) Independent Study Jossey-Bass

HAMMOND M and COLLINS R(1991) Self-Directed Learning Critical Practice Kogan Page

HENDERSON E S and NATHENSON M B (Eds)(1984) Independent Learning in Higher Education Educational Technology Publications, Englewood Cliffs

HOLT J (1976) Instead of Education Penguin Books

KEETON M T and Associates(1976) Experiential Learning Jossey-Bass

KNOWLES M(1975) Self-directed learning: a guide for learners and teachers Association Press

KOLB D A(1984) Experiential Learning Prentice-Hall

KOLB D A, RUBIN I M and McINTYRE J M(1984) Organizational Psychology, A Book of Readings (2nd Edition) Prentice-Hall

LEWIS R(1990) Open Learning and the misuse of Language: a response to Greville Rumble Open Learning 5(1) 3-8

LEWIS R and SPENCER S(1986) What is Open Learning? Open Learning Guide 4, Council Educational Technology, London

LYNCH A J(1925) Individual Work and the DALTON PLAN G. Philip and Son Ltd

NATION D, PAINE N and RICHARDSON H(1990) Open Learning and misuse of language: some comments on the Rumble/Lewis debate Open Learning 5(2) 40-45

PAINE N (Ed)(1988) Open Learning in Transition, an Agenda for Action National Extension College, Cambridge.

REVANS R W(1980) Action Learning Blond and Briggs, London

ROUSSEAU J J(1974) Emile (Translated by B. FOXLEY) Dent, London

RUMBLE G(1989) Open Learning, distance learning, and the misuse of language Open Learning V4 (2) 28-36.

SCHON D A(1987) Educating the Reflective Practitioner Jossey-Bass

STEPHENSON J(1987) Student Controlled Learning in Higher Education, Unpublished collection of papers, North East London Polytechnic

WEIL S W and McGILL I (eds)(1989) Making Sense of Experiential Learning: Diversity in Theory and Practice The Society for Research into Higher Education and Open University Press

CHAPTER 12

MANAGING EXPERIENTIAL LEARNING: THE LEARNER'S PERSPECTIVE

by

JANE HENRY

Introduction

Experiential learning comes in various forms, each of which may have different implications for the management of learning. Elsewhere (Henry 1989, 1990a) I have suggested one can distinguish at least eight different approaches to experiential learning. Fig 12.1 offers a graphic presentation of the methods they use, which together cover just about every learning method known to man bar lectures and rote learning.

Despite their diversity practitioners of such methods often claim common goals, (Henry 1988). These include a desire to develop the person and his capabilities, and to offer a form of learning that emphasises what people can do rather than merely what they know. Advocates of experiential approaches typically share a distaste for more traditional passive methods of instruction such as lecturing, where the student's task is primarily to digest and regurgitate information. Two features seem to distinguish experiential learning, a determination to involve the student personally and to produce a practically useful outcome. Involving the student personally usually means giving the student more control over the topics studied. Delegating control puts more responsibility on the student and presents them with various learner management issues. Aiming for a useful outcome often presents the student with decisions as how to approach the 'learning', again presenting learner management issues.

Types of experiential learning

In terms of their implications for learner management of learning I think it is helpful to think of four very different orientations to experiential learning: Personal development, Prior learning, Placement, Project work.

Personal development

The personal development approach usually focuses on affective development and uses a process of reflection as its route to empowerment. Practitioners typically employ a two stage model of experiential learning where an experience is followed by discussion and the learner is expected to articulate the nature of the experience and discuss the meaning of that experience for him, generally with or in the presence of others. This may involve talking, writing, imaging or expressing feelings non-verbally. Talk based approaches use group discussion or pair based work such as assertiveness training and co-counselling. Writing may involve the use of autobiography or a diary. Imaging may be done alone and involves visualisation, mental rehearsal exercises or part work, where sub personalities are given a voice. Non verbal expression may use art, music or the body as a vehicle. Assessment may well be undertaken by peers and the outcome is often more confident human beings who are more aware of who they are and what they want.

Fig 12.1 EXPERIENTIAL LEARNING METHODS

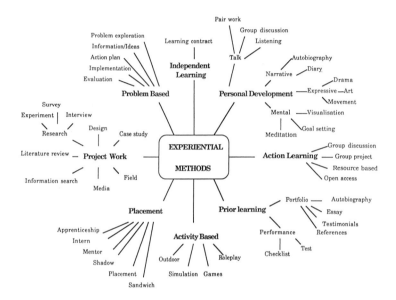

Prior learning

Prior learning may initially attract those who wish their skills to be accepted. This involves the accreditation of previous work or life experience towards an educational qualification. To access the credibility offered by qualification participants are asked to present their case in a reasoned way. Often the student develops a portfolio documenting his existing skills and in the process identifies areas where further learning would be helpful. In practice prior learning often has a personal development component, but the primary route to personal empowerment is via recognition of existing strengths and making good areas where the learner is less skilled or knowledgeable.

Placement

Placement focuses on the practical application of skills and knowledge. The process respects practitioners and encourages competence in students via variants on the idea of apprenticeship.   Perhaps the largest placement scheme in the UK has been the various Training Agency schemes from YTS on, which offer young people on the job training.   Where participants are allowed to participate actively rather than merely shadow someone, learners claim a sense of accomplishment and considerable satisfaction from a feeling of being useful to others; this is in addition to a greater understanding of what is involved.

Project based learning

Project based learning aims to develop autonomy. Projects offer the student choice in the topic area and places responsibility on the learner to devise a plan of action, seek out relevant material, organise it, and present it. The activities concerned may focus round research - for instance surveys or experiments; they may involve a search for information using literature reviews, desk research or interviews and design projects may involve building something tangible or just planning the design. In essence this method is the one used in independent study and problem based learning and all these approaches typically ask the student to go through a similar series of stages. Ideally students end up capable of managing their own learning.

Fig 12.2 and Table 12.1 illustrate some of the differences in orientation in each of these approaches to experiential learning (Henry 1992b).

Fig 12.2   SCHOOLS OF EXPERIENTIAL LEARNING

Capability			Competence
	Presentation		Peer
		PROJECT	PERSONAL
		PLACEMENT	PRIOR
	Practical		Portfolio
Competence			Credibility

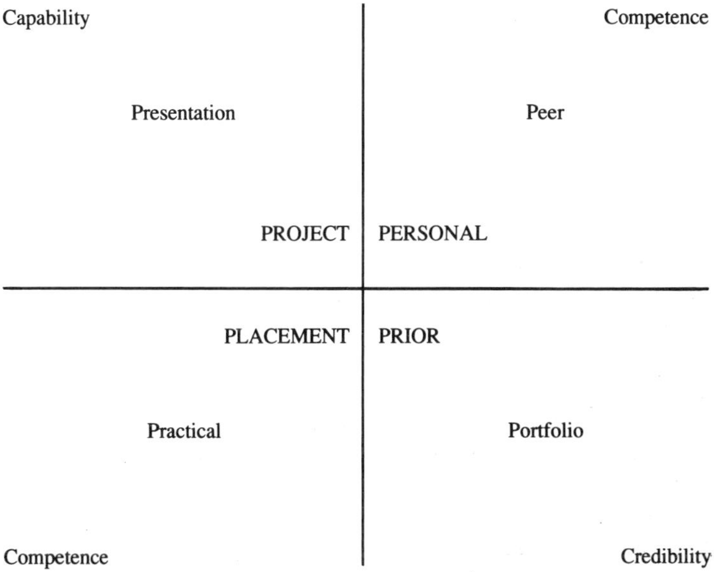

Table 12.1   FEATURES ASSOCIATED WITH EXPERIENTIAL LEARNING
               SCHOOLS

Approach	Project	Personal	Prior	Placement
Concern	Autonomy	Affective	Acceptance	Application
Process	Responsibility	Reflection	Reason	Respect
Method	Presentation	Peers	Portfolio	Practical
Outcome	Capable	Confident	Credible	Competent

Implications for Learner Managed Learning

Each of these approaches generates associated management issues.

Project work

Extensive research at the Open University (Henry, 1979, 1984, 1989b) suggests that
the problems associated with learner management of projects are related to the
process of carrying out a project not project type. Thus for example whether or not
students were trying to do an experimental, design, survey, case study, field,
literature or information search type of project a large percentage of students
seemed to be held back in their learning by human management problems rather
than the content. Furthermore these process related management problems apply to
students regardless of discipline, i e the same issues occur in science, social science,
humanities, education and technology.

Each stage of the project seems to throw up quite different kinds of problem as
indicated in Table 12.2. Briefly anxiety seems to be a major problem at the outset.
Time management features more strongly during the information gathering stage,
and appropriate focus during the final stage of writing and presenting the material.

Table 12.2 Stages of project based learning and associated management problems

Choosing project	Anxiety
Collecting information	Time management
Writing up	Focus

Anxiety

At the outset students are often troubled by anxiety, partly because many have not
tackled a larger piece of work but also because they are unsure of what is involved.
A conventional tactic might be to offer students a list of possible topics so as to
give them a clearer idea of what is expected. Self directed learning advocates have
objected to this idea on the grounds that this diminishes students responsibility.
Comparative studies at the Open University suggest that very few students (less
than 6%) opt to do one of the suggested topics, preferring instead to investigate one
of their own choosing. People orientated teachers may feel a face to face

discussion is essential. Many people argue that it is quite impossible to offer project based learning without face to face support. Our studies suggest an early tutorial where students can see that they are not the only ones to be unclear and anxious about the project along with a tutor on hand to spell out what is required and answer questions is very helpful and much appreciated by those OU students who value and seem to need face to face interactions. (Only around around 50% of Open University students attend tutorials on conventional OU courses, the figure is higher for project based courses.) Paradoxically students are also chronically over-ambitious in what they intend to achieve and tend to pick their topic area out of interest rather than feasibility. Our studies suggest that topic area and scope is often crucial. A young and inexperienced teacher may wish to encourage the student to follow their own interests, more experienced project facilitators take a much firmer line and state clearly where they think the topic is too large and vague and more important likely to be unachievable in the time available. Feasibility has to be as important as interest. Here the tutor's judgement can be critical. In Schools of Independent Study the extended timescale may allow sufficient time for students to discover this the hard way, for themselves.

Time management

Remarkably our studies not only suggest common problems at each stage of project based learning, but that students spend a roughly similar proportion of time on each of these stages, regardless of the discipline, project type or overall time allowed. And in most projects students spend around half their time collecting data. A number of things can go wrong at this stage, but the principal problems are once again ones of project management rather than inadequate data. The classic mistake is to underestimate the amount of time that will be involved in waiting for data - for government departments to reply, for books to arrive in the library, to arrange an interview and so on. This seems to be partly naivety and a self centredness, that expects the world to jump and the materials needed to arrive when required. So over half of our initial 4000 sample failed to get enough data simply because they had not left enough waiting time. This kind of advance planning is often not required in other educational modes, essays can be done just before their deadline by burning the midnight oil, but the waiting time in projects can not be curtailed.

Almost as problematic is the danger of side tracking, a student gets absolutely fascinated by the data they are uncovering, often putting in way above the numbers of hours formerly allotted to the task, but much of this material is not relevant to the project and cannot be used at the end of the day. In a world with unlimited time this might not matter, but our students in this quandary found their other course work suffered or they had left not enough time to revise for the exam and with hindsight wished they had had more foresight and curbed their enthusiasm with more realism.

Focus

Writing up the material was seen by most of our students as the most difficult stage. Sample reports are valued, even though the student's topic may require a very different kind of report, their inclusion seems to give students a clearer idea of the scope and coverage expected, than a verbal description by tutors.

Many students find it difficult to start organising a mass of data. The Open

University studies suggest some form of draft report is less daunting and helps students begin the process, while providing the tutor with a chance to comment on progress. This draft report is best non-assessed, as the student then feels freer to admit the doubts and uncertainties he needs advice cn, than in an assessed piece of work. Another problem students have is a reluctance to leave information out, a maximum word length forces the student to decide which are the more important points. Tutors may also also need some management. Clearly it is vital that they mark the student for the way they have tackled the topic rather than the outcome, the process and not the product.

Paradoxically though this is seen as the most difficult part of the project, tutors and one third of students agreed that their project work was generally of higher quality than standard essay assignments. Students feel more ownership of project work hence they are prepared to put more effort in.

Personal development, placement and prior learning also generate learner management problems, the same issues of anxiety, time management and focus appear but in different ways.

Personal Development

In personal development the relationship between the facilitator and the learner is particularly critical. Fashions change as to the most appropriate means of affective personal development, for example more confrontative methods of the 1960 and 70s, eg encounter marathons and EST have been replaced with less confrontative methods of the 80s such as loving relationship training and co-counselling. The zeitgeist may well be slowly learning a wisdom here, as some research suggests that it is clients of confrontative therapists who report the most negative outcomes from therapy, (eg Yalom and Lieberman 1971). Here anxiety may have offered a useful warning to learners who were not suited to such methods.

Often facilitators advocate the same mode of personal development for all students, ie lets all try meditating, co-counselling or assertiveness training though some particular styles of facilitation suit some learners better than others. Ideally one would attempt to match appropriate training to patterns and stages of development in the learner. Most modes of personal development present an expert helper and a rather helpless client who is done to. There are are exceptions Neuro Linguistic Programming for instance, offers the delightful spectacle of content free dialogue in which the `therapist' has no idea what the client's presenting problem is. Co-counselling avoids the therapist-client inequality by pairing two `clients'.

I suggest that what is required is a much more active role on the part of the student, not just in recognising where they need to develop, but to judge if the approach suggested and more particularly the facilitator involved, and the particular interventions they offer, are working for the learner. This means developing or listening to often subtle or intangible intuitive judgements, and asking questions like does this feel right and listening for a meaning beyond whether the experience is pleasant or unpleasant. It may well suggest offering a number of approaches and facilitators for students to sample and then encouraging and allowing the students to focus on which is right for them. Equally important is a more humble role for the teacher in accepting the learners' judgement as to what is best for them.

In educational institutions most personal development is largely based round talk. In the informal sector much of the purely talk based routes to developing human potential have been superseded by body orientated therapies, such as rebirthing and bio-energetics or subtle energy use. Little of this seems to have filtered across to education except perhaps relaxation classes; management is an exception in that it recognises the value of outward bound training. Outward bound shares some of the elements of initiation rites in that it demands a physically scary and arduous performance from the learner, it also offers this in a group context and usually engenders a strong team spirit and a care and concern for members of the group, so the group will wait and encourage members who are scared of, say abseiling, helping them to achieve the task and overcome their fear. This achievement gives successful learners a sense of confidence which appears to transfer to other environments.

Placement

Placement can be a very powerful experience partly because the student often feels useful. Students on placements are often given very little support, and a sink or swim philosophy may operate for all practical purposes. Amazingly many students do seem to rise to the occasion; perhaps they are bolstered by the trust and responsibility placed in them, and perhaps less inhibited in a new setting with few significant others. Students and staff acknowledge that such work experience can bring out a competence in participants that surprises the students themselves.

However unsatisfactory placements, for instance where the student feels used as cheap labour, just unwelcome or unable to please, can become dreadfully negative experiences that demotivate participants appallingly. Ideally students on placements would be supported during the process and where there seemed no hope of overcoming an unsatisfactory placement withdrawn.

Prior learning

Managing prior learning might sound more straightforward yet this path too present problems that need managing. Many prior learning programmes ask the students to examine and justify their skills in some detail. This kind of self scrutiny can produce unexpectedly strong emotional reactions in students, for the process forces students to come to terms with who they are and what they know. While the realisation that one possesses previously unthought of skills, from say childrearing, offers a boost, the wider issue of examining yourself to work out what these skills are and what you want is a threatening exercise. It is no accident that many such programmes offer considerable 'counselling' and peer support.

Conclusion

All these approaches aim to empower individuals. A satisfactory outcome is more probable if the facilitators involved take steps to ensure that the experiences are fulfilling and productive. This is more likely if teachers attend to the problems associated with the process of taking part in these experiences and offer measures to help overcome them. Our studies of the project based method suggest that a combination of simple measures go a long way towards increasing the percentage of students who find the experience useful and worthwhile. These include judiciously timed moral support, appropriate warnings, concrete indications of what is required and formative assignments to ensure progress. (Henry 1990a elaborates.) It has also been implied that there may need to be a further shift in the power base between teachers and learners, which would encourage learners to determine whether they are ready for the experiences suggested or not and if the methods and facilitators advocated were working for them. I suggest that teachers and learners could usefully pay more attention to the idea of readiness and nurturing. Readiness in the sense of whether it is right for the student to undertake this particular form of experiential task with that particular facilitator at this time. Nurturing in the sense of attending to the potential fragility of psyches and developing support mechanisms that mitigate feelings of failure when students do not achieve what they set out to, whether with a project, in their personal development, on placement or via prior learning.

REFERENCES

Henry J(1979) A study of project work at the open university, In <u>Proceedings of the Association of Institutional Researchers Annual Forum</u>

Henry J(1984) Project exercises in a research methods course. In Henderson E and Nathenson M (eds) <u>Independent Learning in Higher Education</u>, Educational Technology Publications, Englewood Cliffs

Henry J(1988) Experiential Learning: an international survey, <u>TCC Report no 58</u>. IET Open University

Henry J(1989) Meaning and Practice in Experiential Learning, in Weil S W and Gibson I(Eds), <u>Making Sense of Experiential Learning: Diversity in theory and practice</u> , SHRE/Open University Press

Henry J(1990) The Human Side of Project Work, in Farmer B,Eastcott D and Lantz B <u>Aspects of Educational Technology XX111: Making Learning Systems Work</u> ,Kogan Page

Henry J(1990) Developing human potential experientially in Winterburn R(Ed) <u>Aspects of Educational Technology XXIV: Recognising Human Potential</u> Kogan Page

Yalom I and Lieberman M(1971) A Study of Encounter Group Casualties, <u>Archives of General Psychiatry</u>, vol 25 p16-20

CHAPTER 13

CAN LEARNERS MANAGE?

By

Tyrrell Burgess

Komensky and Learner-Managed-Learning

Three hundred and fifty years ago, Jan Amos Komensky (Comenius) arrived in England to advise on education. The English were at the time preparing for civil war, regicide and dictatorship, so his visit was brief, and his advice was not taken for two decades and then only in part. The event is of interest for three reasons. First it reminds us that ideas always travel and thought seldom respects boundaries. Komensky's connections with England are a case in point. The works of John Wyclif were brought to Prague by Czech students who had been at Oxford, inspiring the great Jan Hus whose followers established the church of which Komensky became bishop. He himself was directly influenced by the new view of knowledge and learning set out by Francis Bacon. In turn, two more Czech students, this time at Cambridge, told Samuel Hartlib about Komensky, leading to the invitation and visit of 1641. This visit, brief though it was, is part of the intellectual link between Bacon's `House of Solomon' and the foundation of the Royal Society(Young,1932). I myself believe that Komensky's educational theory and practice greatly influenced also both the political theory of the radicals in the English revolution and the development of British empirical philosophy.

The second interest Komensky holds for me lies in the ideas he put forward. In many ways he is the most enduring of all the great educators. To read his <u>Great Didactic </u>(Keatinge,1896) today is to stumble, again and again, on topical issues. He believed in, and provided for, universal education: his text books were best sellers all over Europe for 200 years. His pedagogy was designed for mass application, and he faced the problems this created. He was the first, perhaps the only, really democratic educational theorist. His system would accommodate everyone; rich, poor; clerics, labourers; girls, boys; clever and stupid. Until the end of the vernacular school, at the age of twelve, he would educate them together: `it is therefore undesirable to create class distinctions at such an early age, or to give some children the opportunity of considering their own lot with satisfaction and that of others with scorn` (Keatinge,1896). He wanted education to be efficient and offered a means for making it so. A good grounding in the vernacular, for example, would enable children to learn Latin in two years, Greek and modern languages in one year and Hebrew in six months. He saw clearly that mistaken education made people stupid.

The key to his method lay in his view of the individual. A child was a rational creature - the image and joy of the creator. Education was what helped a child to rise to full human dignity. It was not a matter of adapting the child to the environment: the individual and individual talents were to be respected. All capacities were ripe for development, not merely the academic. An apt education was apt for individuals, and learning took place best through the activity of the learner. Here the new science flowed through Komensky's humanity: children were to learn through the senses, through evidence, not on authority. Above all, they were to be encouraged to question their teachers, to learn not just from their teachers but from each other. It is sobering to recall that his mission to the children and students of the world began at Fulnek, just 20km south of where the Second Learner-Managed-Learning conference took place.

The third way in which Komensky's international fame is of relevance to us is in his relating of theory to practice. Much of his vision is shared by educators today: few have matched his capacity to turn it into reality. He himself was conscious of developing new theories, rooted in what was known then about children, about how they grew and matured and about how they learned. He hoped to establish a science of education, alongside the other new sciences. His theories of education are always related, by analogy, to the processes of `nature'. But he never advances a theory without following it with a proposal. This is so, he says and we should thus do the following. The question Komensky asks of educators, today as in his own day, is this: if you think that education can be improved, what do you propose should be done - and why should you think that your proposals are more likely than others to beat the stubborn resistance of traditional educational practice?

Many people share a view of education which holds that learning takes place best when the learner is active, rather than through the busy activity of teachers: that there are many achievements, not measurable by tests and examinations, that are of value and should be encouraged and recognised; that the world is enriched by developing all the myriad interests, talents and energies of individuals, not treating pupils and students as little pitchers to be filled by Gradgrinds with facts by the imperial pint, as circus animals trained to do trivial and demeaning tricks or as instruments of state, of `society' or the economy. Our solution is `learner managed learning': Komensky's implied challenge from across the centuries is - can learners manage? How can we enable them to do so? What will persuade the world that they have learned? I hope, in this paper, to offer the outline of an answer to this challenge.

A Framework for Learner-Managed-Learning

For learner managed learning, or personal responsibility for education, or independent study, we have to create, I believe, a framework of practice and theory. This framework will differ in detail according to circumstances, to prevailing educational traditions and habits, to the age of the pupils or students, to the availability of teachers and to national or more local laws and regulations. There are, however, seven elements which seem to me to be essential. These are a planning period, time for private study, effective tutorial arrangements, access to specialist tuition, schemes of validation and accreditation, and a convincing theoretical base. In describing these briefly I shall draw on experience in England in establishing such a framework in schools (Burgess and Adams,1985) , in colleges(Burgess,1977) and in professional development (Adams and Burgess,1989).

Planning

If learners are to manage, the first thing they need is time and occasion to plan. They need to be encouraged to reflect on their present position, on what has been their experience hitherto, on their achievements and qualifications - on what, in short they themselves bring to the enterprise of education. They, the learners, are education's greatest resource. They must know what that resource is, so that their educators may know too. Next they need to ask what is problematical about the position in which they find themselves: what more is required, what needs remedy, what lack must be supplied. Solutions to these problems, proposals to learn more, or something new or different, to strengthen existing knowledge or skill, to improve professional or personal capability, become in effect the student's educational programme. Time is required for this because if done seriously, such planning is taxing. Where the activity is unfamiliar, students take time to feel at ease with it. Their first thoughts often turn out to be insufficient or mistaken. Many take time to develop trust in the process: they have been so much at the mercy of curriculum and syllabus in the past that they look for a hidden curriculum now, trying to guess what their educators 'really want'.

Moreover, no planning can be done in a vacuum. A student's solutions to educational problems are constrained by what is available. Not all solutions are possible. In this sense the planning takes on an aspect of negotiation, where the student discovers what is available - may indeed reformulate the problem so as to attract a readier solution. This too requires time.

With students in higher education, it typically takes half a term to produce a viable programme which will form the basis of their education for the next two or three years. For students in secondary school preparing for the two years before the statutory leaving age, Elizabeth Adams and I proposed that the planning should be developed throughout the preceding year(Burgess and Adams,1985). In English primary schools, where pupils may plan their own activities for a part of the week ahead, the period may amount to an hour. What is important is that time, occasion and formal requirement should be provided, so that students know what is required, think seriously about it and trust the system to accommodate their proposals.

Private Study

The next requisite is private study. If learners are to manage, they need time to pursue their own inquiries, write up their own findings, conduct their own experiments. They need time to monitor their own progress, reflect on their achievements and make immediate plans. They cannot do this if every moment is filled with instruction, the attempt to cover an external syllabus, or if any free time is filled with prescribed work. (Interestingly Komensky proposed a fairly short school day of four hours, even for older children, to allow for private study as well as recreation). It is in periods of private study that genuine concentration becomes possible. In normal school and even college classes the demands of a timetable, not the interest or importance of the topic, determine when attention is broken off. In some school and college systems changes of classes are so regular and frequent that little concentration is possible, which partly accounts for the inefficiency of much educational practice.

In higher education, it is frequently assumed that students will work on their own, outside formal classes, but the practice (in contrast to the repetitious extension of classwork) is virtually unknown in secondary schools. In neither do students have the opportunity to manage their own learning, to be masters not the slaves of their educational programmes, to show responsibility rather than mere responsiveness. The question is what the balance should be between formal classwork and individual work -that is, work which directly contributes to the successful completion of a programme negotiated and agreed as a solution to the student's educational problems. Experience suggests a third of the total time needs to be reserved for genuine private study if a learner is to manage learning.

Effective Tutorial Arrangements

Both the planning period and private study depend upon the third element of the framework: effective tutorial arrangements. Every student should have a personal tutor who has responsibility for the student's educational programme, development and achievement. This responsibility should remain throughout the student's stay in the institution. It is through the personal tutor that the student negotiates and plans a programme, then carries it through by agreed means, including private study, to a successful conclusion. Where private study is supervised, the tutor supervises - and is thus quickly alert to any student's faltering or demoralization. Problems with specialist studies can be discussed, and remedies proposed. Weaknesses in general learning skills can be tackled, morale maintained, pitfalls avoided. Above all, the tutor offers that continuity of personal relationship upon which education depends. (Komensky thought that having too many different teachers confused children and led to inefficient education).

The task of the tutor is threefold: to create confidence, to give access to what is available in the institution and to maintain quality. Confidence is required if students are to face their problems, propose solutions and follow these through successfully. No student can do this without help in knowing and understanding what the institution has to offer, let alone negotiating an appropriate share of it for the chosen programme. The maintenance of quality is a duty not only to the students, but to society at large. This is not just a matter of testing and examining, though some students may wish to be measured in this way. It is mainly a question of applying professional judgment to those achievements which are not testable and examinable, but which everyone agrees to be of the essence of a good education: in creativity, competence, capability and cooperation.

Whether or not such tutorial support is offered will depend on the organization of schools and colleges. Time and occasion could be made for it. In higher education in England the idea is familiar if the practice is sometimes etiolated. In schools examinable subjects are so dominant that personal tutors normally have at best a `pastoral' rather than an educational function, and in only a few schools is tutorial time effectively provided and used. The suggestion, made earlier, that tutorial time might usefully be combined with supervised private study offers one solution. Experience suggests that if every teacher in a secondary school, regardless of formal status, were to have a tutorial responsibility, it would be possible, with present staffing levels, for each to be tutor to twenty students. If these students stayed with one tutor through the school, this would imply tutor groups made up of four students from each of the five years.

Specialist Tuition

The fourth part of the framework is specialist tuition. The division of knowledge into subjects is venerable: it derives at the latest from Aristotle. Many (including Komensky) have been suspicious of it, and advances in knowledge are frequently made between rather than within subjects. But this is how education has come to be organised. The system of examinations, the requirements of governments, the organization of schools and the careers of teachers are all based on bodies of knowledge. This is the way in which knowledge is present to the young. It may be that a better way might some day be found, but meanwhile what students need is not an argument but access to what is. In other words, it is irresponsible to talk of 'deschooling' society or to advocate the destruction of the academic bureaucracy. The inevitable passivity of learners in most education systems must be tackled directly rather than as a consequence of the (unlikely) overthrow of all existing practice.

The subject offers a coherent view of knowledge, a discipline for dealing with it and a body of qualified practitioners to advance and explain it. These are critical advantages. The students can know something, they can appreciate what they do not know, they can know more of knowledge by knowing of many approaches and they can understand that, whatever we know, human ignorance is boundless. This knowledge, these disciplines can be made available to learners. Learner managed learning does not scorn them: on the contrary. Nor does it mean that students study chaos if they feel like it, relate everything to themselves alone, abjure evidence and objective standards or remain trapped within their own prejudices. Rather it means that students face the rigour of subject disciplines as part of an agreed educational programme which has its own coherence and rigour.

This requires, not that subject departments are destroyed or weakened, but that they organize themselves so as to accommodate the serious requirements of students. These may often be met by lecture courses, seminars and classes of the familiar kind. For most purposes students will require very similar provision. It is the exceptions who will ask for more flexibility - but it is just this that many teachers have found the most rewarding part of their task.

It is possible here only to indicate the kind of organizational change that would make this possible. Broadly it is that the division of the school or college timetable into forty minute or hour long periods should be replaced by larger blocks of time within which a department might organize large or small group teaching or individual tuition, depending on the calls which students made upon it after a considered period of negotiation and planning.

All the arrangements which have been described so far have been within schools and colleges. It is possible for institutions to make such changes, and some have. Change is seldom popular, however, with those who are not making it and may not understand it. Things like syllabuses and examinations, which are so familiar as to seem to constitute the whole of education, have almost automatic public assent. Innovation does not. The history of education is littered with good ideas and practice which withered because they gained no general recognition.

Validation and Accreditation

Two devices are needed as part of a framework for learner managed learning. One is a device for assuring the learners that the programmes they have agreed are worthwhile, that it would be `valid' to devote a significant part of their lives to following the programmes to a successful conclusion. Of course, under a developed scheme of learner managed learning they will have gained the agreement of their teachers, but experience suggests that both teachers and learners welcome and benefit from some external assurance.

For example, we were proposing to introduce a scheme of independent study in an institution, a polytechnic, in which all new courses needed the scrutiny and approval of an external body - the Council for National Academic Awards (CNAA)(Burgess,1977). The traditional means of gaining such approval was by submitting descriptions of the course, including syllabuses, timetables, schemes of work, reading lists, assessment arrangements and so on. None of these were available for a scheme in which each individual student would create an individual programme. To overcome reasonable suspicion, we proposed an external `validating board' which would scrutinise the proposed programmes (on a sample basis, though all were available) and say whether or not the judgment of the staff in agreeing these programmes was satisfactory. This satisfied the CNAA. What we had not foreseen was the difference the validating board made within the institution. Its discussions were critical in helping the staff to establish standards and conventions in running the scheme. Its presence, impending and actual, raised the seriousness and confidence of students. It helped to reassure colleagues in other departments of the propriety of the innovation. It made possible the grant of public recognition for individual programmes of independent study of the same standing as all other courses in higher education.

A similar device was pioneered in secondary schools, in the scheme referred to earlier(Burgess and Adams,1985) , to enable the governing bodies of schools to validate' the individual programmes of students for the last two years of compulsory education. In all forms of learner managed learning the learners respond with confidence when they have an external assurance that what they have planned is indeed worthy of support.

Record of Achievement

They also need recognition of their achievement when they finish. This is granted at the end of most courses by the qualification attained, and these qualifications have always attracted public recognition. Those managing their own learning might well decide to work for such qualifications: those wishing for particular careers may find themselves compelled to do so. The difficulty is that working for and succeeding at academic tests and examinations, though universally recognised, does not constitute the whole of education or even for many people the most important part of it. In England in 1984 the Secretary of State for Education announced a policy for introducing `records of achievement' in secondary schools, in order to record and give credit for those achievements of students which were not measurable by tests. It seemed to me then that unless some way were to be found of recognising these achievements the records would not be worth the paper they were written on. The difficulty was to find a way of giving the records more than local currency. The young owners of the records, their parents, employers and the public at large must be able to believe in the records. They must have confidence that any achievements described were real and any standards claimed had actually been reached. They had to believe in the probity of the process by which the records were produced and in the objectivity of the descriptions they carried. What was needed was a device which could match examining bodies as a guarantee of confidence.

The device we tested with a group of schools(Burgess and Adams,1985) was that of an `accrediting board' in each local education authority (which maintains the schools) whose duty was to report on the process by which records were produced in each school and, if all was well, to give accreditation. The work of these boards was itself overseen by a national `accrediting council for education'. This experience suggested that it would be possible to establish national arrangements of this kind without high costs or an inflated bureaucracy. This solution was apt for the particular circumstances of the introduction of records of achievement. Other solutions may be needed on other occasions. What is not in doubt is that where learners are managing their own learning, they need not only the assurance of a validating process that their programmes are worthwhile but that of an accrediting process that their achievements are honestly and realistically reported.

Theoretical Underpinning

The final requirement for learner managed learner is unlike the others. They are the necessary practical steps. This last is the theoretical basis. There may be some who question the need for such a thing. After all, education is a practical matter: it either works or it does not. Innovators may often find that sympathisers and opponents alike are impatient with philosophy. There are three reasons why theory is necessary. The first is that all practice implies a theory. Indeed practice is often theory based, even if the theory is no longer well remembered or understood. People like to think there is a rational basis for their behaviour and will usually assume that there is one even if they cannot quite say what it is . This means that they do not judge a new proposal on its merits, but in terms of their current practice and presuppositions. The new proposal, if at all radical, cannot win that argument. It is important therefore to make explicit the theory behind existing practice, to contrast it with the new theory and so make it possible to shift the ground of the argument.

For brevity's sake, I shall risk putting the contrast very crudely. There have been many great educators and many findings of educational psychology which, however different - even incompatible - they may be, have united in the view that learning best takes place when it derives from the initiative and activity of the learner. Learner-managed-learning honours this insight, embraces it and builds upon it. Our claim is that it is in accord with the best expressed and best developed educational theory, and one which as is at least as venerable as any other.

Current educational practice is inspired by a quite different principle: that learning depends upon the initiative and activity of the teacher, reinforced often by the whole apparatus of state. Of course, in practice the contrast is less stark. Individual teachers may well go on behaving as if the first theory were true, even where the second is officially enforced. Even nations where individualism has seemed entrenched may have spasms of assuming that a Secretary of State should do everything and, worse, that nothing should be done unless he does it. It seems clear, however, that we should do better to incline towards the first theory and develop practical expressions of it. Learner managed learning is one of these.

I also believe that there is something which we can call the logic of learning(Popper.1980) . Of course, the ways people actually learn are as various as people, and they have been described and catalogued. It is useful, even so, to look at the logic of it. Learning starts when we are faced with a problem, maybe a disappointed expectation or a frustrated desire. We proceed by trial and error. We have a hunch, a theory, a solution, which we try out. If it fails we try again. If it succeeds we make do with it until it in turn disappoints or frustrates. I would wish to assert baldly, again for brevity, that we do better if in our educational institutions we act in accordance with the logic of learning rather than against it. Learning begins with problems, not with instruction. Instruction is best thought of as a solution - so the question at once arises as to what problem it is a solution to. Is it in any sense a problem of the learner?

I wrote earlier of expectations and desires. The disappointment of the former raises problems of what is or is not the case, and these are typically problems which academics seek to solve. Most people are concerned with the other kind of problem, those that arise from frustrated desire. They want to do something, to get from one state of affairs to another, and find they cannot. Faced with these problems they turn to education, only to find educators preoccupied with solutions to the first sort. These may indeed help a bit, but often they inhibit a practical solution. In being so committed to instruction educators deny themselves the pleasures of listening and learning.

My conclusion is that learner-managed-learner accords with what is securely known about human learning, with the logic of learning and with the urgent problems of people the world over.

I end with a parable. Once upon a time there were two psychologists who thought to rig up a contraption in which they placed two litter-mate kittens(Held and Heim,1963). This contraption was such that one kitten could move about relatively freely, while the other was suspended in a cradle or gondola and thus had no independent movement. The cradle was attached, via a pivot, to the free-moving kitten. The latter would jump about and be active and by doing so would swing the gondola kitten round in its cradle. The kittens were kept in the contraption like that for several hours a day, but otherwise were placed with their mother in darkness.

After some weeks of this the kittens were given little tests. One of these was to place each kitten in turn on a narrow shelf with an easy drop on one side and an intimidating drop on the other. (The latter had a glass shelf across it to prevent hurt.) What the psychologists found was that the active kitten always chose the easy drop: the gondola kitten stepped off either side at random. I draw the conclusion that in order to learn about the world and to master their environment the animals needed to be active. The gondola kitten was swung about and saw much the same things as the active kitten but, being inactive, had not been able to make sense of them. It had learned nothing of importance, certainly nothing that would save it from a nasty jolt.

Traditional educational practice, which requires children and young people to follow only prescribed courses set by someone else, makes `gondola kittens' of them. They are swung about in front of innumerable facts and experiences, but they are not active: they do not initiate anything. It is not surprising that they learn little of importance. One attempt to remedy this is learner managed learning.

REFERENCES

Adams, E and Burgess, T(1989) Teachers' Own Records, NFER - Nelson

Burgess, T(1977) Education After School, Gollancz Burgess, T and Adams, E(1985) Records of achievement at 16, NFER - Nelson

Held, R and Heim, A(1963) `Movement-produced stimulation in the development of visually guided behaviour', Journal of Comparative and Physiological Psychology, No.56

Keatinge, M W (Translator)(1896), The Great Didactic of John Amos Comenius, A & C Black

Popper, K R(1980) The Logic of Scientific Discovery, Hutchinson, 10th impression revised

Young RF (ed)(1932) Comenius in England, Oxford University Press

CHAPTER 14

THE TEACHER IN SELF-DIRECTED LEARNING: MANAGER OR CO-MANAGER?

By

Joy Higgs

Introduction

A difficult question facing tertiary educators today is how to design and conduct educational programmes which promote learner self-direction and also maintain a level of teacher control. This paper addresses this question.

There is a considerable amount of debate in the educational literature relating to the concepts of freedom and control in education, and the way these concepts are manifested in educational programmes. It is argued in this paper that freedom in learning can be equated with responsible learner self-direction and that control, meaning the direction and management of a learning programme, can be the role of both teacher and learner.

The optimal state for learning involves a balance of freedom and control in the learning programme. This is particularly applicable in learning programmes which occur within educational institutions. Here, some form of teacher control of the learning programme is inevitable. This paper explores the necessity and desirability of such control and examines the place of teacher and student control in such learning programmes.

The definition of self-directed learning being used here is as follows: Self-directed learning is an approach to learning in which the behaviour of the learner is characterised by responsibility for and critical awareness of, his or her own learning process and outcome, a high level of autonomy in performing learning activities and solving problems associated with the learning task, active input to decision-making regarding the learning task, the use of the teacher as a resource person and learner interdependence with teacher and co-learners.

Freedom and control in the educational literature

Freedom in and through education is an important theme in the educational literature. It is inherent in the concept and practice of liberal education where the development of the individual's potential is seen as a fundamental goal of education (Gamson et al, 1984). Similarly, humanistic education is ultimately a process of facilitating the development of self-actualised individuals (Rogers, 1969,1975). Gamson and colleagues (1984) introduced the term "liberating education" to refer to education for critical awareness leading to empowerment. A similar view of liberating education is presented by Freire and Shor (1987) in their book "A pedagogy for liberation" which continues Freire's long advocacy of education which liberates people both socially and politically. The focus of this view of liberating education is offering students the opportunity to think critically about the limitations to their freedom and thereby helping them to learn to be free.

A common term used to describe control in educational programmes is structure. Structure can be defined as "the supporting or essential framework" and "the manner in which a complex whole is constructed, put together or organically formed" (The Concise English Dictionary, 1982). This definition contains both a description of structure and the idea of structuring as a dynamic action which includes initial design and ongoing implementation elements. Structure in education is a necessary part of the teacher's role and responsibility to provide learning programme management.

Philosophically freedom is linked to initiative, responsibility, participation and feelings of freedom (Schofield, 1972). Freedom of the individual can be defined as the relative or complete exemption from outside control of that individual. This includes freedom of the individual's choice, will, actions, learning and development. Control of (or over) the individual is the relative or complete limitation of the freedom of the individual. In the educational setting teachers have traditionally held and used power and influence.

When seeking to provide learner freedom in real situations it becomes evident that no programme is exclusively characterised by freedom or control. It is also found that freedom itself has inherent and circumstantial limitations which necessitate the introduction of some control to avoid the problems which arise when an increase in freedom or a removal of authority is sought. This control can be provided by external sources such as a teacher or the environment, or by the individual who seeks freedom purposefully. Thus, the ideal situation is to seek (within the constraints of the existing conditions) to achieve a balance between freedom and control, giving consideration to such factors as the learning goals and the ability of the participants to cope with and implement changes in freedom and control.

Balancing freedom and control

Freedom and control can be seen as a continuum. At one pole of this continuum lies freedom or "licence". In extreme cases this could be described as anarchy. Many people in this situation have a desire for order or control. At the authority pole, people feel restricted and they desire freedom. The position of balance of these two extremes is "controlled-freedom". It is characterised by a level of individual freedom made possible by (and occurring within) a framework of control.

The polar positions can be compared to the common images of didactic teacher-dominated education and laissez-faire (open) education. In the first case, individual student freedom is denied and students may well feel frustrated or stifled and wish for greater freedom. In laissez-faire education, the level of freedom is high but the (potential) negative consequences (e.g. confusion and lack of purpose) may prompt students to ask for direction, or to behave in such a way as to demand the attention of authority figures.

It can be argued that in education and society in general, endeavours by individuals to move away from the polar positions, can be problematic. For instance, overthrowing external authority does not guarantee the capability of the newly-freed individuals to direct or govern themselves. They may well indulge in conflict amongst themselves, or on a personal level, become as confused as people existing at the licence end of the continuum. Similarly, moves of individuals or groups away from the licence pole can result in the establishment of a dictatorship situation. In a sense, such moves, associated with the inability to handle the consequent changes effectively, can result in even more extreme positions than before. The path of effective moves away from the constraint or licence positions towards the balanced position, is characterised by planning, and preparation of individuals to ensure their ability to cope with the ensuing changes.

This discussion has a number of implications for teachers. For instance the desire of students for greater freedom, or the desire of the teacher to allow students greater freedom, does not guarantee that students (and teachers) can cope with the consequences (such as increased uncertainty) of this greater freedom. The move toward the desired goal needs to be planned, balanced and monitored to avoid a swing too far in the opposite direction. To avoid this, it would be advisable for the participants in the learning programme to reflect on the advantages and disadvantages of changes and effects occurring at various stages as they move along the continuum. Following a move to a desired position, the task of maintaining the delicate balance between freedom and control at that point may not be easy. The teacher for instance, as the authority figure, may seek greater security by becoming more authoritarian or he/she may find it difficult to determine what level of freedom a student can handle.

Freedom and control in self-directed learning

The following sections outline a Theory of Liberating Programme Systems which is derived from doctoral studies conducted by the author (Higgs, 1989). This research examined elements of freedom and control within self-directed learning programmes conducted within several health science tertiary education programmes in Sydney. The research strategy comprised three parallel modes of inquiry: abstract conceptualisation and reflection based on available research and theoretical literature; empirical study of learning programmes involving self-directed learning(incorporating a survey of two groups of students and their teachers engaged in independent learning programmes); and reflections on the researcher's personal experiences as a self-directed learner and as a teacher of self-directed learners.

The project resulted in the development of an emerging middle range theory which comprises a set of constructs and inter-related propositions. This theory illuminates the nature and practice of self-directed learning. Further investigation is required to test the robustness of the theory.

The thesis contained in this theory is that independent learning programmes can be structured in ways that promote or liberate self-directed learning behaviours. Inherent in this argument is a dialectic relationship between elements of education related to the concepts of freedom and control. Kolb (1984) defines a dialectic relationship as: "mutually opposed and conflicting processes, the results of each of which cannot be explained by the other, but whose merger through confrontation of the conflict between them results in a higher order process that transcends and encompasses them both" (p.29).

It is argued that elements related to freedom and control occurring in independent learning programmes, can be merged to develop a higher order process which can be referred to as controlled freedom or as a liberating programme structure or system. (In the latter case the learner is a co-manager of the learning programme.)

Self-directed learning

Three major constructs were defined in the theory: self-directed learning, learner task maturity and learning programme structure. "Self-directed learning" was defined at the beginning of this paper. The study identified self-directed learning as a dynamic and developmental phenomenon, with learners growing in their independent learning abilities. It is inappropriate to say that individuals are either self-directed learners or they are not. Instead they could be described as ranging from highly self-directed or independent, to highly dependent learners.

A highly competent self-directed learner is a learner who is capable of exhibiting the following characteristics: a readiness for autonomous learning, attitudes of responsibility and self-reliance, purposive independent and interdependent action in relation to the learning task, productive and power-sharing relationships with other people in relation to the learning programme, effective use of learning and cognitive strategies (including metacognition and critical reflection) and a state of mind which involves self-awareness and self-evaluation. In addition, the highly competent self-directed learner achieves, as a result of these behaviours, further development as a self-directed learner and changes in conceptions and personal meaning. Beyond these general characteristics, competence in self-directed learning is also context- and content-specific. This is dependent for instance, upon the learner's past experience of similar learning tasks, and his/her ability to implement learning strategies appropriate to the context and content of the learning programme. This is a reflection of the learner's task maturity.

Learner task maturity

The construct "learner task maturity" represents the level of readiness and ability of the learner to deal with demands of a specific learning task at a given time. This construct was developed to reflect the willingness and ability of learners to play a responsible and self-directed role in a given learning situation, and their ability to respond flexibly and appropriately to the demands of the learning situation.

Thus, there is both an attitude and ability component to learner task maturity. The ability aspect relates to cognitive style/preference characteristics, the effectiveness of the learners' general learning styles and approaches to learning, and more particularly to the learner's readiness for self-directed learning. The attitude element of learner task maturity is seen as having both personality aspects (e.g. field independence, curiosity) and experiential aspects (e.g. responses to previous experience with independent learning programmes). Learner task maturity is specific to different goals/tasks, relates to past learning experiences and learning skills, changes over time as the learner's abilities develop, and can be enhanced by teacher input.

Learning programme structure

"Learning programme structure" refers to the dynamic framework within which the participants in a learning programme operate. This is a "complex whole" in which numerous environmental, task, social and individual dimensions need to operate congruently to optimise learning opportunities and outcomes. A "Liberating programme system" is a learning programme structure developed through the co-operation between teacher and learner(s) and in which there is mutual decision making.

Theoretical propositions

The following sections outline the theoretical propositions contained in the Theory of Liberating Programme Systems.

> PROPOSITION ONE: The teacher's role in independent learning programmes is that of overall programme manager.

The role of the teacher as a manager of independent learning programmes involves making decisions based on evaluation and diagnosis of the capabilities of the student and of the demands of the learning task, and on an ongoing monitoring of the student's performance and progress. The success of this role rests firstly upon the teacher's understanding of self-directed learning and familiarity with the demands, limitations and opportunities of the learning context involved, and upon the development of an approach to managing self-directed learning programmes which is consistent with these. It also includes helping to prepare students with low learner task maturity for the demands of their learning programmes. This can involve specific guidance or assistance with new skills (e.g. research strategies) that students need to learn for their learning projects.

> PROPOSITION TWO : Management of independent learning programmes by the teacher can result in the creation of programme structures which liberate learners' self-directed learning or which restrict such learning, or in the case of joint programme management the result is a liberating programme system.

This proposition is a development of a theory of liberating structure presented by Torbert (1978). In this theory Torbert contends that "to educate toward shared purpose, self-direction, and quality work, an ironic kind of leadership and organizational structure, which is simultaneously educative and productive, simultaneously controlling and freeing, is necessary" (Torbert, 1978, p.113).

In essence, this proposition presents two arguments. The first is, that the teacher can influence conditions under which the student is learning and thus the nature of the experience (and the level of autonomy) the learner achieves. Secondly, it argues that in determining the learning conditions, the teacher has a major influence on the extent to which the learner is also able to influence these conditions.

As overall manager, the teacher can actively guide the learning programme and provide a liberating programme structure for the learner. In this case the learner has limited direct input to the design and management of the programme structure. As learners become more competent as self-directed learners they are more able to and desirous of, directly influencing the programme structure. Where the learner is capable, it is appropriate for the learner to take over (all or much of) the programme management, in which case a liberating programme system occurs. In this situation the teacher retains the overall management and delegates much of the implementation management to the student.

> PROPOSITION THREE : A learner's self-directed learning behaviour at any point in an independent learning programme is a function of the interaction of several key factors including: - the learner's task maturity,
>
> - the opportunity available to the learner to be self-directed (including the opportunity to make choices/decisions regarding the programme),
>
> - the learner's goals for the learning situation,
>
> - the nature of the framework (e.g. boundaries) set for the programme,
>
> - the nature and demands of the learning task,
>
> - the extent to which the programme goals and format are acceptable to the learner (i.e. Is the learner agreeable to pursuing these goals in this manner?), and
>
> - the learner's choice of mode of behaviour in the given situation.
>
> PROPOSITION FOUR : Learners (and teachers) in independent learning programmes can be regarded as purposive subsystems. Where this purposefulness is combined with competence as a self-directed learner, student management of the learning programme is desirable.

Independent learning programmes can be thought of as systems in which teachers and learners are autonomous, "purposive subsystems" (Moore, 1973). As such these individuals are capable of making choices based on their perceptions of environmental/system conditions and performing actions to achieve their goals. Also such individuals behave in a way which reflects their individual personality. Personality in this sense is a reflection of the individual's knowledge, intention and familiarity with the choice situation (Ackoff and Emery, 1972).

The concept of the individual as a purposive system was a valuable addition to this theory. It encompasses the idea of freedom and autonomy in learning which is a major element of contemporary literature on adult and self-directed learning (e.g. Boud, 1988; Brockett and Hiemstra, 1991; Brookfield, 1986; Candy, 1991; Hammond and Collins, 1991; Taylor, 1986;) and re-emphasises the important role of the learner as a decision-making, goal-directed agent. It also stresses that learners are purposeful and that learners who see themselves as being capable of managing their own learning programmes would prefer to be proactive rather than reactive.

> PROPOSITION FIVE : In a liberating programme system the learner(s) and teacher share control over the programme (including sharing the decision making and power).

This proposition emphasises the sharing between teacher and student of power and decision making. Such sharing is a reflection of Boud's (1988) argument that interdependence is an essential element of autonomy in action and is a stage beyond independence. "In this view independence, being independence from a teacher or authority figure, is a stage through which learners need to pass in any given context to reach a more mature form of relationship which places them in the world and interrelating to it rather than being apart from it" (Boud, 1988, p.29). Another aspect of power sharing is that the programme structure becomes explicit. In practice there may still be unstated expectations on both sides. However, there is much to be said, particularly if we are talking of a state of teacher/learner interdependence, for clearly communicating about the conditions of the learning programme structure.

> PROPOSITION SIX : Programme structures/systems which facilitate or liberate students' self-directed learning behaviour, are characterised by a balance of FREEDOM and CONTROL.

Freedom within the programme structure relates to opportunities the learner has to be self-directed and the level of open-endedness which characterises the programme. Control in the programme structure refers to the boundaries and direction(s) which limit and guide the programme. The structure of learning programmes should be seen as a dynamic balance of freedom and control and the effects this can have on learner behaviour. Within an environment of controlled-freedom the learner's behaviour also becomes characterised by both control and freedom or responsible self-direction. As learners become increasingly competent as self-directed learners, they take on the role of providing and managing controlled-freedom as part of their behaviour, instead of simply responding to the controlled-freedom provided by the teacher.

> PROPOSITION SEVEN : The nature of the learning programme structure or system should be contingent upon or matched to, a number of contingency/situational factors such as: the learner's task maturity, the nature and demands of the learning task, the learning programme's goals, the learner's goals, the learner's readiness and preference for managing his/her own learning programme.

The idea of contingency management is strongly supported in management literature (Fiedler, 1964; Hersey and Blanchard 1982). This proposition is an adaptation of contingency management theory to the management of independent learning projects. In the empirical investigation conducted in this research project different modes of self-directed learning behaviour were identified in relation to different types of programme structures. For instance, during the preliminary phase of their programmes, a programme structure characterised by security, manageability of task and ongoing contact between teacher and learner, was associated with exploration, experimentation and risk-taking learner behaviours.

> PROPOSITION EIGHT : Mismatch between the programme structure/system and the contingency factors (particularly learner task maturity), and lack of congruence between elements of the learning programme can result in the occurrence of "Restricting Programme Structures". This term refers to programme structures which restrict or limit the student's self-directed learning behaviour.

Proposition 2 contended that teachers can create programme structures which restrict student learning. This proposition extends this argument by relating this restriction to a lack of congruence between the management and nature of the programme structure, and contingency factors such as learner task maturity and the nature of the learning task.

> PROPOSITION NINE : To be successful (and liberating), learning
> programme structures/systems need to be dynamic since they need to adapt
> to the changing demands of contingency factors and changing perceptions
> of the learner(s).

This proposition is consistent with Taylor's (1986,1987) landmark research on
patterns of self-directed learning experiences from the learners' viewpoint. In
Taylor's study, learners' behaviour patterns changed (in phases) according to major
reorientations in the learners' perspective on knowledge, learning, authority and
themselves.

For instance, when learners were faced with challenges to their expectations and
assumptions as a result of their experience they became disoriented, until such time
as they were able to comprehend and name the problem they were facing. Another
phase described by Taylor was reorientation. This involved private reflection which
resulted in major insights or synthesis of ideas and the development of a new
approach to the learning task.

> PROPOSITION TEN : Congruence of the elements in a learning
> programme structure/system enhances the success and "liberation effects"
> of the programme.

Congruence between the elements of a learning programme can be created by
choosing to teach on the basis of a certain educational philosophy and/or conceptual
framework. In such a conceptual approach, the word "congruence" (in relation to
the elements of the programme), refers to the aim of ensuring consistency between
the teacher's actions, the teacher's expectations of the student, the learner's
expectations and the learning conditions created.

This idea is strongly associated with Torbert's (1978) ideas of authenticity of the
teacher's behaviour and accountability of the teacher. A similar argument is
presented by Griffin (1980-81) who stresses the need to achieve congruence
between our (the teacher's) values and techniques. Likewise, Argyris and Schon
(1974) address the question of congruence between espoused theories and theories
in action.

Conclusion

In self-directed learning programmes students would be expected to experience
greater freedom than they would in teacher-directed learning programmes.
Teachers involved in self-directed learning programmes are faced with the task of
coping with a new role and providing a new type of control, in order to foster the
learner's freedom. Nash (1966) describes the teacher's dilemma as follows:

> If the teacher provides too much guidance and leadership, if he tells the pupil
> everything he needs to know, if he exercises an indisputable and weighty
> authority, the pupil is liable to find himself on a path with the sun in his eyes,
> blinding him and preventing him from picking out the route for himself. On
> the other hand, if the teacher gives no guidance or leadership, if he tells the ...
> [learner] nothing, and makes him find his own way unaided, the ... [learner]
> finds himself on the same path, this time in total darkness, without even the
> minimal light necessary to see his way (in Schofield, 1972, p.273).

Ideally self-directed learning should be placed between the two positions described by Nash. In self-directed learning programmes, the teacher needs: to provide enough light for the learner to see that alternative paths and goals exist, to be willing to help the learner make these choices, and to walk along with the learner discussing his or her journey. How far the teacher lets the learner wander astray or stumble around in pockets of darkness and how much help the learner seeks, is decided by the travellers. Such decisions make each journey unique and can make each phase of the journey different from the last. This is compounded by the effects of the journey on the development of both teacher and learners and by the influence of other travellers met along the way.

The theory of liberating programme systems presented here has moved beyond the picture of the teacher who walks along beside the travelling learner, as a guide and facilitator of self-directed learning, to a point where both travellers are purposeful learners and both participate in decisions about the journey. Each one is a navigator and may even shape the road that is travelled.

REFERENCES

Ackoff R L and Emery F E(1972) On purposeful systems, Tavistock Publications, London

Argyris C and Schon D(1974) Theory into practice, Jossey-Bass, San Francisco

Boud D(1988) Moving toward autonomy, Chapter 1 in Boud D(Ed) Developing student autonomy, (2nd Ed) Kogan Page, London

Brockett R G and Hiemstra R(1991) Self-direction in adult learning, Routledge, London

Brookfield S D(1986) Understanding and facilitating adult learning, Jossey-Bass, San Franscisco

Candy P C(1991) Self-direction for lifelong learning: A comprehensive guide to theory and practice, Jossey-Bass , San Francisco

Hayward A L and Sparkes J J(Ed)(1982) Concise English Dictionary, Omega Books Ltd, London

Fiedler F E(1964) A contingency model of leadership effectiveness, Pages 149-190 in Berkowitz L(1964) Advances in experimental social psychology, Volume 1, Academic Press, New York

Freire P and Shor I(1987) A pedagogy for liberation, Macmillan Education , Basingstoke

Gamson Z F and Associates(1984) Liberating education, Jossey-Bass, San Francisco

Griffin V(1980-81) Self-directed adult learners and learning,in Yearbook of Adult and Continuing Education, (6th Edit.), Pages 501-507

Hammond M and Collins R(1991) Self-directed learning: Critical practice, Kogan Page, London

Hersey P and Blanchard K(1982) Management of organizational behaviour: Utilizing human resources (4th Ed), Prentice-Hall, Englewood Cliffs

Higgs J(1988) Planning learning experiences to promote autonomous learning, Chapter 2 in Boud D (Ed) <u>Developing student autonomy</u> (2nd Ed), Kogan Page , London

Higgs J(1989) <u>Programme structure and self direction in independent learning programmes</u>, Unpublished PhD Thesis, University of New South Wales, Sydney

Kolb D A(1984) <u>Experiential learning - Experience as the source of learning and development</u>, Prentice-Hall , Englewood Cliffs

Moore M G(1973) Toward a theory of independent learning and teaching, <u>Journal of Higher Education</u>, 44, 661-679

Nash P(1966) <u>Authority and freedom in education</u>, John Wiley and Sons, Chichester

Rogers C R(1969) <u>Freedom to learn</u>, Charles E Merrill, Ohio

Rogers C R(1975) The interpersonal relationship in the facilitation of learning, Chapter 1 in Read D A and Simon S B <u>Humanistic education sourcebook</u>, Prentice Hall,Englewood Cliffs

Schofield H(1972) <u>The philosophy of education</u>, George Allen & Unwin, London

Taylor M(1986) Learning for self-direction in the classroom: the pattern of a transition process, <u>Studies in Higher Education</u>, 11, 55-72

Taylor M(1987) Self-directed learning: More than meets the observer's eye, Chapter 14 in Boud D and Griffin V (Eds) <u>Appreciating adults learning: from the learners' perspective</u>, Kogan Page, London

Torbert W R(1978) Educating toward shared purpose, self-direction and quality work - the theory and practice of liberating structure, <u>Journal of Higher Education</u>, 49, 109-135

CHAPTER 15

A "CONSTRUCTIVIST" THEORY OF ACQUISITION, AND

ITS IMPLICATIONS FOR LEARNER-MANAGED-LEARNING

By

Don E Tinkler

" ... the gulf between the mature or adult products and the experience and abilities of the young is so wide that the very situation forbids much active participation by the pupils in the development of what is taught. Theirs is to do - and learn... that which is taught is thought of as essentially static. It is taught as a finished product, with little regard either to the ways in which it was originally built up or to changes that will surely occur in the future. It is to a large extent the cultural product of societies that assumed the future would be much like the the past, and yet it is used as educational food in a society where change is the rule, not the exception."

John Dewey

Introduction

The above statement is from John Dewey rather late in his career. By 1938 he had realized that his theory of experience had become distorted by the "progressives", and in defence of his position wrote <u>Experience and Education</u>. As might be expected, he rejected the notion that knowledge can be imposed upon students as in traditional schooling. Surprisingly however, he was also quite vigorous in his rejection of "progressive" education:

"The problem for progressive education is: What is the place and meaning of subject-matter and of organization <u>within</u> experience?" [Dewey's emphasis]

On the cover of the 1963 edition of the book, immediately below the title, the following publisher's note appears:

The great educational theorist's most concise statement of his ideas about the needs, the problems, and the possibilities of education - written <u>after</u> his experience with the progressive schools and in light of the criticisms his theories received. [ed. emphasis]

In the book he makes the important claim that not all experiences are genuinely or equally educative (1938:27):

It is not enough to insist upon the necessity of experience, or even the activity in experience. Everything depends upon the <u>quality</u> of the experience which is had." [again, Dewey's emphasis]

In the context of discussions on "Learner-Managed-Learning" we could well reflect upon those words of Dewey written more than fifty years ago. But, before proceeding to the specifics of "managed" learning, we might look again at "learning" per se. Questions worth asking would be: What happens in the process of learning? What conditions optimize the process? What are the implications for the learner and for the teacher?

Once those questions have been addressed, we can move on to consider appropriate new measures, and the stage in the education/schooling continuum at which the measures might be initiated to shift from conventional school practice towards learner-managed-learning as an alternative .

Recent years have seen classroom teachers, disenchanted with traditional theory, attempting to improve their professional effectiveness by adopting a range of innovative strategies such as experiential learning, inquiry learning, problem solving, cooperative group learning, and negotiating curriculum with students.

"Constructivism", a development within cognitive psychology, provides the supporting rationale for each of these innovative approaches to learning. Further, constructivism supports the importance now being attributed in education to self-esteem and "metacognition" - awareness of the learning process - and is consistent with the conclusions of research into novice-expert representations of knowledge... but, more on that later.

This chapter will be divided into three parts. The first part will report the investigative phase and the generation of a constructivist theory of knowledge acquisition. The second will explain how the modelling has been applied to curriculum design and development, with special application to the area of social education. This will be illustrated by reference to the <u>Humanities Core Curriculum (HCC)</u> chart and <u>A "Futures" Perspective</u>, the recently published handbook for the teaching of social education in Australian primary schools. In the third part I will suggest some implications to be drawn from the project and related research for learning and teaching at a variety of specific levels, as well as for the period before a child is old enough to be accepted for formal schooling. Throughout I will draw attention to the links between my work over the past decade or so and learner-managed-learning.

I will be an attempt to bridge the gulf referred to by Dewey in the opening quotation, and to answer his question as to the place and meaning of organization <u>within</u> experience. It will be an approach which avoids the excesses of traditionalism at one end and progressivism at the other, and yet which incorporates the best of both, offering new freedom for learner and teacher alike.

PART 1: T0WARDS A THEORY OF MENTAL ABSTRACTION
As a teacher in the late 1960s, I had seen the reported conclusions of Jean Piaget, that children are not just adults in miniature, as a break-through in educational thinking. His theory of "stages" of cognitive growth and "equilibration" seemed to signal a revolution in the way educators might look at such things as intelligence.

Piaget never claimed to be a teacher, believing his contribution to education to be as a genetic epistemologist - not as a pedagogue. It was left to others to draw out the implications of his work for learning and teaching.

What seemed to be needed in this model was something of a quantum leap to enable movement from one stage to the next. Piaget offered "equilibration" as a self regulatory mechanism that would lift a child from, say, the pre-operational stage to the concrete operational stage, at around seven years of age. However, by 1979, when presented with the challenge to develop new curriculum in social studies, I came to see that this raised all manner of questions. What would be an indicator that equilibration had taken place, or was about to take place? Once equilibration had occurred, would the child be at the same stage in spatial awareness as in, say, ability to understand higher-order inference in language?

In the mid seventies I had begun to toy with the idea of "mental abstraction" as describing the activity of the brain/mind in dealing with sensory input. The theory was still in a comparatively early stage of refinement when in a thesis in 1982 I offered a simple illustration to explain the notion.

A very young child experiencing the family cat for the first time becomes aware of the object, the cat, as her sense receptors inform her of a bundle of "cat" sensations. Such sensations as colour, shape, proximity, feel, smell and sound are received by the sense receptors and recorded by the brain/mind as percepts. Further experience of the cat reinforces those percepts and an "identity" is attributed by the mind to the object from which it is reasoned the bundle of sensations emanated. The identity I will refer to as "cat". So far in this example "cat" applies only to the family cat. The child reasons that this identity is "cat", but that identity (e.g. "pillow") is not "cat".

In the event that, at a later stage, the child observes a different object producing a similar set of sensory input, say, the Persian from next door, her mind becomes active on the new percepts, matching them and comparing them with her original identity we might call identity A, "cat", establishing a new identity B, "cat", and by a process of abstraction forming the category "catness" - a first-level abstraction. So it is with further objects producing similar percepts, the tabby or the ginger cat that crosses the garden; all are subsumed under the category "catness" - still a first-level abstraction.

Some time later the same child might observe a tiger in a circus or at the zoo. Until she becomes aware of the dissimilarities between the tiger and those objects that she has subsumed under "catness", it is likely that she will group the new object under "catness", along with the family cat, the tabby and the Persian.

However, once the percepts inform her of the startling differences between what she has previously experienced and what she is now experiencing (for example, the object is larger by far and makes a loud growling noise), the new identity may be seen as belonging to "tigerness", a new category. That category can be subsumed under the extended category "catness" - a second-level abstraction - which can now include domestic cats, tigers and later, lions, leopards, pumas and jaguars. Depending upon the capacity for mental abstraction, the child might retain "tiger" simply as a separate identity until experience of further tigers produces a greater elaboration and the category "tigerness".

In a similar way the identity "dog" and the category "dogness" are formed from the percepts through the process of mental abstraction as the mind sorts through the percepts, comparing analysizing, and classifying. In a variety of ways both objects and established categories can be grouped and regrouped. From the categories "catness" and "dogness" can be formed eventually the notions of "animalness", "mammalness", "marsupialness" and "livingness", higher-level abstractions generated by the mind as it becomes active on the variety of sensory experiences.

It is in the identification of characteristics of identity and in the organizing of categories that language can play a vital part. Whorf (1956), Vygotsky (1962), Ausubel (1968) as reported by Novak (1977), and Novak himself each stress that language plays an important role in mediating higher levels of cognitive functioning. However, it is asserted that even without language labels, at the early or elementary stages, the mind is capable of generating a series of higher-level abstractions. Identities enable recognition of individuals, but both identities and first level abstractions can be regrouped to be subsumed under new higher level categories. If an identity cannot be subsumed the percepts may be used to establish new categories. Sometimes a subsumed identity is extracted from one category to be included in yet another new category. An identity may be seen as a cat, a pet, an animal, a nocturnal creature or a living thing, depending upon the capacity of the mind and the requirement for mental abstraction.

Some idea of the relationships between identities, levels of abstraction, categories and extended categories is provided in the following diagram (Fig 15.1):

Fig 15.1 A HIERARCHY OF MENTAL ABSTRACTIONS

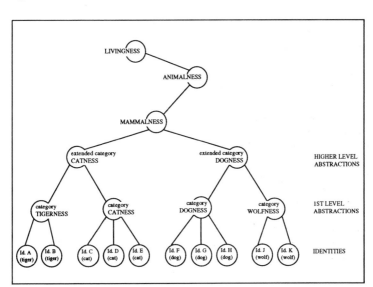

What should be said at this point is that a child's category "catness" would be qualitatively different from that of most adults. The more experiences (either first hand or vicarious) the more elaborated can be an identity, and the greater will be the capacity to construct or reconstruct categories. To put it another way, a veterinarian will have a different mental representation of "catness" from that of, say, the non-veterinarian/ non cat-owning conservationist concerned about the destruction of small native fauna in the Australian bush by feral domestic cats.

The Place of Experience

To talk of sensations and percepts is to talk again about experience, for it is from experience that the mind generates percepts, and from those percepts, categories, constructs and concepts.

The description of the mind active in a process of mental abstraction at a very early age is congruent with the contention of Paul Brandwein (1977) that "the child comes to school with a comprehension consisting of a world of constructs, which we know to be somewhat faulty. But he comes, nevertheless, with an idiosyncratic way of learning".

It is the task of the teacher to discover that idiosyncrasy, to help correct the faults in those constructs, and to provide order and a reduction in the complexity of the developing mass of information, so the child will gain increased comprehension about his/herworld.

Piaget and Cognitive Growth

Having briefly presented the theory of "mental abstraction", let me return to the factors Piaget saw as affecting cognitive growth. They were:

　　　　　1)　　　　Nervous maturation

　　　　　2)　　　　Experience

　　　　　3)　　　　Social transmission

　　　　　4)　　　　Equilibration

The theory of "stages" and "equilibration", as presented in the 1960s, produced a revolution in teaching - the practice of schooling. Teachers accepted that they should provide experiences and then await the child's progress through the "stages" which were considered to be invariant in order, but which may vary with individuals as to time of appearance. They were encouraged to allow students to proceed at their "own pace", and to promote "peer interaction" as the best form of classroom learning. The message to teachers seemed to be quite clear: Do **not** intervene, do **not** attempt to advance children through the stages. The message transmitted to parents was also clear: Do not force the children, and leave the teaching to those who know, the teachers at school.

Looking back, we as educators created yet another myth, and that myth is sustained even today. Perhaps Piaget was a victim of historical circumstance. May-be educators made more of Piaget's theories than he had intended.

Bob Samples, author of <u>The Metaphoric Mind - A celebration of Creative Consciousness,</u> tells of the impact in the United States of the Launch of "Sputnik" in 1957. The immediate response was to call education to account for what was considered a national "disgrace". In the words of Samples (1976:54):

A massive educational-guidelines conference of blue-ribbon scientists and educational elite was held in Woods Hole, Massachusetts in 1958. Jerome Bruner, who guided the government's involvement through the fateful Woods Hole conference, was the mentor. And the school of thought he mented was authored by Piaget. Piaget came off the shelves at Woods Hole.

Piaget visited the United States in 1964 for the "Jean Piaget Conferences on Cognitive Studies and Curriculum Development" held at Cornell and Berkeley. He was accompanied by Eleanor Duckworth, a former student, who acted as translator.

The impact of the visit was immediate. Its significance can be measured in the hundreds of research projects it stimulated in universities and the material it produced for colleges of teacher education, not only in the United States, but in countries all over the world. The statements of 1964 are still being presented in teacher training institutions as representative of the views of Piaget about "stages" and cognitive growth.

However, it is important to stress that Piaget continued to write, researching and modifying his views, for a further sixteen years. A Dutch researcher, Rita Vuyk (1981), reported of her study of Piagetian ideas at Geneva that Piaget had become "less and less interested in stages", and had introduced a new term, "reflective abstraction", which he considered to be so close to equilibrium as "to seem the same mechanism described in two different languages and from two points of view".

The "Supportive" Model, An Alternative to Piaget

The theory of "mental abstraction" is essentially "constructivist". It is asserted that we each construct our "reality" through mental abstraction, the processing by the brain of sensory input. The reality is dependent upon both the range and quality of the sensory input or experiences: a limited experience results in a limited reality, a broad range of experience generates an elaborated reality.

Piaget's 1960s theory I refer to as the "autononous" model - autonomous, because growth was determined by "equilibration", his invented term for a self-regulatory mechanism which acted to correct any disequilibrium brought about by new experiences, and which raised an individual to a higher "stage" of cognitive growth. It was also equilibration which led him to his notions of "assimilation" and "accommodation".

In developing an alternative "supportive" model of cognitive growth, I have discounted Piaget's "stages" in favour of the idea that the growth is continuous, though irregular; the irregularity being influenced by four factors:

1)   The total state of the brain and the central nervous system;

2)   the level and the quality of experience;

3)   the level and the quality of social interaction; and

4)   "sound pedagogy" (the art/craft of teaching - some-thing that can be applied by a parent, a peer, or some other person, as well as the professional teacher)

I point out in the comparison that in the alternative model equilibration is no longer needed, since the process of cognitive growth can be more parsimoniously explained as due to the activity of mental abstraction.

Some Implications to be drawn from the "Supportive" Model

Factor 1) **the total state of the brain and the central nervous system:**

From what limited understanding we have of how the brain functions, we can say that no person operates at a constant level of efficiency. Chemical imbalance, physical or emotional trauma, fatigue, boredom, illness, drugs, hunger and dehydration, can contribute to changes in brain efficiency. Not that classroom teachers can do much about the state of the brain, but they can make allowances for the fluctuations, and in the case of trauma can intervene sensibly to reduce some of the impact.

Factor 2) **the level and quality of experience**

Recalling the statements of John Dewey on the importance of experience, it is suggested that in the contrived environment of the classroom teachers should select experiences largely on the criteria of quality.

Educators should try to establish the level of student prior experience - being prepared to compensate for those who may lack a rich experiential background - before contriving a teaching experience.

Factor 3) **the level and quality of social interaction**

In recent years there has been an increasing concentration upon self concept as being important to effective learning. Of major importance in the development of positive self concepts are the kinds of relationships that have already developed in student personal social interaction in groups, whether that might have been within the family, among peers, or with children and teachers in previous classes.

Classrooms are by nature busy places. There is such a variety of factors operating; so many things going on simultaneously; so much that is completely unpredictable; decisions to be made immediately; events that are very public, some embarrassingly so - both for students and for teachers; and each of the human elements enter with a personal background and contribute to a class history that is completely unique. In spite of the "busy-ness", care should be taken to establish a climate built on concern for and a warm acceptance of each member, a classroom climate in which honesty, open-ness and mutual trust can develop.

Factor 4) **"sound pedagogy" (the art/craft of teaching)**

In searching for a term to describe teacher-intervention, vital to learning, I had hoped for something that would identify teaching more as an art than a science. The dictionary term "pedagogy" defined as "the science or profession of teaching; also, the theory or the teaching how to teach" was the nearest approach to the descriptor I was seeking.

"Sound pedagogy" is much more than "instruction". In applying sound pedagogy the teacher's task extends beyond simply providing and managing experiences. The role of the teacher expands to include all of the following:

        1)   selecting experiences using "quality as a measure of appropriateness;

        2)   organizing,timing, monitoring and managing the experiences;

3)   providing order in the experiences presented (giving consideration to scope and sequence in what is developed and presented as curriculum);

4)   attempting to reduce some of the complexity of the material or information being presented (The world for both children and adults is indeed complex, but if some of the complexity is reduced in presenting ideas initially, the learnings often make more sense when later placed back into their original complexity);

5)   drawing learners into purposeful two-way communication (generating a climate where learners are free to inquire, to explore issues, to formulate questions, to express ideas, to debate points of view, and to seek solutions to problems);

6)   extending the learners' interaction with the learning environment (extending the range and variety of the learning context).

The Teacher and the Learner

If the notions of "constructivism" and "mental abstraction" are accepted, then it follows that, rather than being fully "aware" of the brain activity of the student, the teacher is able only to perceive indicators of what is going on in the mind/brain of the student in the signals transmitted by the student in the teaching-learning exchange.

Depending upon the reading of the student response signals, the teacher attempts to gain optimum teaching success by varying the teaching strategies in accordance with his/her interpretations of the signals.

Novice-Expert Representations

Reported research from the Learning Research and Development Centre at Pittsburg introduces yet another perspective to "sound pedagogy". It comes from evidence regarding the way an educational task is perceived by novices and experts. The Pittsburg research discounts the view that experts simply carry out a task faster, and thus more efficiently. The claim is that the representations of experts are qualitatively different from those of novices. Head of the research centre, Lauren Resnick (1983) suggests:

... the task of the instructor is not to search for ways of presenting information that directly match the thought or performance patterns of experts. Rather it is to find instructional representations that allow learners to gradually construct those expert representations for themselves.

Assuming a continuum with the "novice" representations being to the left and "expert" representations to the right (Fig 15.2), the challenge for teachers would be to find ways of meeting the students where they are along that continuum.

Fig 15.2 THE NOVICE-EXPERT CONTINUUM

Novice Representations — — — — — — — — — — — Expert Representations

Applying "sound pedagogy" the skilled teacher (the expert) would attempt to match the representations of the students (the novices) drawing them forward over time towards more expert representations.One view is that the research offers a new direction for teaching into the future. If we accept that knowledge will continue to grow at an exponential rate, there could be a time when no amount of subject study will keep teachers up to date with the latest developments in their chosen fields. For some teachers this may already be the case.

The evidence suggests that teachers in the future should focus upon the process skills, becoming in fact "experts" in the processes that optimise learning. From such a position of competency, teachers could then become "facilitators" of learning, being prepared to explore new subject content alongside their students. Whether or not the learning-teaching interaction takes place in the formal institutional settings of today, teachers would continue to perform a vital community role into the future.

Although developed in response to what were identified as needs of primary school children, the "supportive" model of cognitive growth - returning the teacher as an important element in the learning-teaching equation - has already been accepted to have value in the teaching of infants and pre-school children, and has also been applied to the teaching of mature adults studying at post-graduate level.

PART 2: THE "LOGICAL SEQUENTIAL" MODEL OF CURRICULUM DEVELOPMENT

The "supportive" model became the basis for the "logical sequential" model for design of curriculum. (Fig 15.3)

Some comments on the Logical Sequential Model:

"HIGHER ORDER LANGUAGE SKILLS" (C) go beyond skill levels accepted for minimum competency in reading and oral and written communication. The need for increased capacities in literal, inferential and critical skills is considered basic to any move towards curriculum improvement.It should be recognised that a level acceptable in 1950 or even in 1980, will fall far short of the literacy needs of students in the 1990s. A range of higher order skills is required so that capacities for mental abstraction can be enhanced, and mental constructions of reality can approach the "ideal". Higher order skill development can begin before a child reaches primary school.

In infant classes children usually spend a great deal of their time in activities building up sensory awareness. Why should not those activities in a modified form be continued through the primary years, supplemented of course by exercises that develop the students' capacity for inquiry, analysis, synthesis, problem-solving, monitoring their own learning, and choosing between options? These are the skills that students need to be able adequately to explore their worlds, attempting to build sound constructions of reality. They are also the skills essential for any programme that involves learner managed learning.

The notions of "mental abstraction" and MENTAL GROWTH lead logically to ideas of "constructivism" in the DEVELOPMENT of CONCEPTS.

The place of QUALITY EXPERIENCES in the construction of sound concepts has already been mentioned.

Fig 15.3 THE LOGICAL SEQUENTIAL MODEL OF CURRICULUM DESIGN

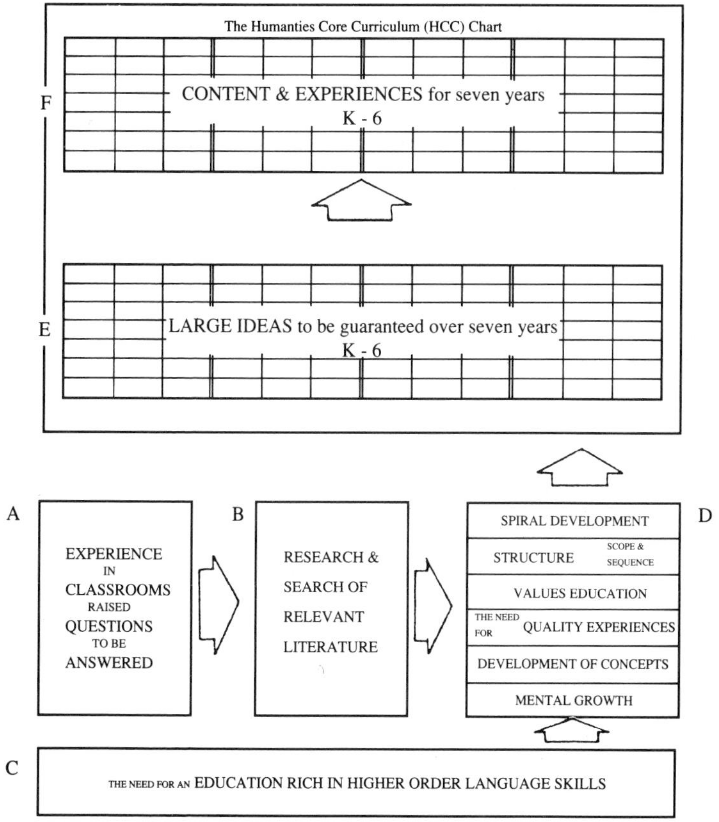

A: Reflection upon classroom practice raised a series of questions which led to:-

B: Intensive research and a search of relevant literature.

C: Arising from A and B an assumption was made that any improvement in curriculum design in social studies would demand an education rich in higher order language skills.

D: From reflection(A) and research (B) six planks were selected each to be placed in sequence, reading in the direction of the arrows, as illustrated.

From that structure was built:-

E: A statement of LARGE IDEAS about social education, set out on a grid to cover the seven years in the primary school.

This in turn led to:-

F: A statement of CONTENT and EXPERIENCES set out on a matching grid to that of E, the LARGE IDEAS.

Because the project concerned curriculum in social education, VALUES EDUCATION needed to be considered. Social education involves discussing values - attitudes, beliefs or feelings of varying intensity, either favorable or unfavorable. Teaching about values is not to be confused with imposition of values. The preferred approach has been to emphasize "values refining", using certain teaching strategies to help students understand how values generate and change, and how they affect judgement and making choices between options.

It was Jerome Bruner (1960) who drew attention to the need for an act of learning to serve in the future. In writing about the importance of STRUCTURE he concluded:

... knowledge one has acquired without sufficient structure to tie it together is knowledge that is likely to be forgotten. An unconnected set of facts has a pitiable half-life in memory. Organizing facts in terms of principles and ideas from which they may be inferred is the only way of reducing the quick rate of loss of human memory.

The top planks (D) were included to draw the theoretical towards the more practical, the actual structure of the curriculum; something that would make the project more relevant to teachers.

SCOPE AND SEQUENCE identified very early in the project as being important in developing sound ideas about society were incorporated in the model, along with a rising and broadening SPIRAL DEVELOPMENT which would allow students to see issues over time from an increasingly broad perspective.

An example of the spiral applying to experiences in social education can be seen in the visits a child might make to a dairy farm; one visit being made when the child is in the first year at school and the subsequent visit some years later when the same child is in Year-six. Although almost overawed by the bustle, the sounds, the smells and the threatening bulk of the animals, the six-year-old child's major impression might be that the cows seemed to know when it was time to be milked and what to do when let into the milking shed. May-be the real interest in the visit was the chance to feed the calves from a bottle.

On the second visit the child is able to build upon the earlier impressions which, very likely, have been supplemented and informed by other experiences such as reading about cattle and viewing videos or films about dairying. Perhaps the class has talked about the things to look for during the visit. While watching the cows being yarded and milked, the child may become aware of certain aspects of the milking process hardly noticed before, taking particular note of the hygiene carried out by the farmhands, the manner in which the cups are fitted to the cows, and the way the milk flows through the transparent pipes into the huge churn where it awaits pick-up by a milk-tanker. What happens to the milk beyond the dairy farm would be a question that could lead to some personal exploration and research.

Each experience, whether personal or vicarious, direct or reported, generates a range of impressions contributing to a total picture. Those impressions, once recorded, are available for recall, to be connected and re-connected with impressions gained from subsequent and future experiences. In this way the child is able to construct mental associations, say, between a visit to the dairy farm and subsequently seeing spray irrigation equipment at a machinery exhibition.

While the mental activity takes place without the intervention of others, the educator - whether parent or teacher - can assist to improve the degree of understanding and help forge new and appropriate mental linkages.

From the above example it will be realized that the construction of the world-picture and world-view is a continuous integrating process, producing chunks of information that may not fit neatly into a particular academic discipline nor that can be restricted to the subject compartments imposed by the traditional school.

So much of the content and experiences provided in formal education programmes lack an integrating factor that could link them with understandings already established. Designers of curriculum should allow opportunities over time for students to "revisit" and build on aspects that have been introduced at earlier levels.

An "Interactive" Social Education Curriculum

The next logical step in the development was to look at the shape a new type curriculum might take. A matrix or grid (E) was proposed on which could be set out the large ideas or concepts to be generated over seven years . That step led to incorporating in the design a further matrix (F), a "twin" to (E) which could carry the CONTENT and EXPERIENCES suggested as being suitable to generate the large ideas or concepts.

The result: the HUMANITIES CORE CURRICULUM (HCC) Chart which is a seven-year matrix of **large ideas** and **content** in social education, carefully selected for their **scope and sequence**, and positioned into twelve **strands** that develop as rising and broadening **experience spirals**. "Social education" for the project was taken to include aspects of anthropology, sociology, economics, politics, the life sciences, applied science, and mathematics as well as the more traditional history and geography.

Set out on the HCC wall chart and grouped into five clusters, the twelve strands or categories were designated as below (Fig 15.4).

The United States National Council for Social Studies (NCSS) Task Force on Scope and Sequence for Social Studies in 1983 recommended an "holistic - interactive approach presenting content in ways that provide a comprehensive view of a complex whole; interactive because everything relates to everything else; holistic because it casts events in their broadest social context".

The report draws attention to the fact that "first graders and Ph.D. candidates in sociology both study the family, but of course, at different levels of analysis". It also suggests that teachers encourage "direct student intellectual involvement through discussion, small group work, student presentations, debate, simulations, brain-storming and independent study". Also noted is that there is "a need to explore the application of brain research and other developmental research to the selection and sequencing of the social studies curriculum".

Fig 15.4 THE SOCIAL EDUCATION CURRICULUM

KEY/ SYMBOL	STRAND	CLUSTER
Ch	CHANGE	CONCEPTUAL CLUSTER
HT	HISTORICAL TIME	
SA	SPATIAL AWARENESS	
SO	SELF AND OTHERS	SELF AND SOCIETY CLUSTER
Co	COMMUNITY	
OS	ORDER IN SOCIETY	
E	ENVIRONMENT	NATURAL CLUSTER
RU	RESOURCE USE	
I	INDUSTRY	TECHNOLOGICAL CLUSTER
TC	TRANSPORT/COMMUNICATION	
M	MARKETING	
WW	THE WIDER WORLD	SOCIAL ECONOMIC GEOG. CLUSTER

As well as being recognized for the research into novice-expert representations, Lauren Resnick is one of the foremost researchers in the field of cognitive psychology. In an article published in 1983, Resnick wrote of the "need for a constructivist theory of instruction". Later in the same article she concluded:

> It now seems absolutely certain that our task is to develop a theory of intervention that places the learner's active mental construction at the very heart of the instructional exchange. ... a constructivist intervention theory must address all the traditional concerns of instructional design: how to present information to students, what kinds of responses to demand of students, how to sequence and schedule learning episodes, and what kinds of feedback to provide at what points in the learning sequence.

The article served to reinforce many of my earlier conclusions and contributed a new influence in the development of what has become an integrated theory of learning and teaching.

Recognized widely as a new paradigm in curriculum development, the HUMANITIES CORE CURRICULUM (HCC) is not a "constructivist theory of instruction" (to use the terms of Lauren Resnick), but a curriculum developed from the application of a "constructivist theory of instruction", a theory which generated out of a careful analysis of research and thirty years of successful and innovative classroom practice.

Designed as a curriculum for life, both in the present and the future, students are brought to a greater awareness of themselves and others and their physical and social environments. At the same time they should gain a range of useful skills which will empower them to operate more successfully within those environments.

Through an understanding of the self one can begin to understand others. Such an understanding then provides the base upon which to construct understandings of the community and, eventually, of the global society. Suggestions of content to build those understandings are further amplified in a new teacher handbook(Social Education For Australian Primary Schools: The Humanities Core Curriculum, A Futures Perspective). Included in A "Futures" Perspective are strategies that will assist teachers to design and implement interesting and challenging integrated classroom programmes.

PART 3: A CONSTRUCTIVIST THEORY OF ACQUISITION AND ITS IMPLICATIONS FOR LEARNING AND TEACHING

The implications of what has so far been presented are quite extensive. They apply very much to learner-managed-learning and offer guidance on the matter raised earlier in this presentation:

Where in the education/schooling continuum should the shift from conventional practice to learner-managed-learning begin? It should be accepted without further argument that we cannot afford to leave the skill building for learner-managed-learning until the years of post compulsory schooling demand their application - as seems to be the present situation. Because those skills of analysis and synthesis take a considerable time to develop, and they in turn depend upon a set of even more elementary higher-order skills, it would seem that the earlier the shift begins, the more effective will be the outcome. Certainly, there is valid evidence that the nurturing of the skills can and should begin long before children move out of the primary school.

Several years ago in Adelaide I was asked by an officer of Australian Radio National what the work might mean for various levels of the schooling process. I have reviewed what I wrote in reply to that question, and present it here re-worked as the general implications to be derived for learning and teaching. Although I have included in the paper suggestions for learning and teaching to upper secondary school level, comments will be limited to lower secondary school and earlier levels.

Some general comments:

There is need for a cognitive theory of KNOWLEDGE ACQUISITION that can become the base for a CONSTRUCTIVIST THEORY OF INSTRUCTION.

Constructivist position (simplistically stated)

The learner constructs his/her own reality (world) from experience, ie. limited experience - limited reality, expanded (elaborated) experience - expanded (elaborated) reality.

> The mind cannot be considered as an empty vessel to be filled with knowledge as one might fill a bucket with water.
>
> The mind is far more sophisticated than any computer yet designed, or even contemplated.
>
> It is natural for the mind to become active on experiences (as natural as curiosity is to children).
>
> Learning is an active process (evidence suggests the process may occur even before birth).
>
> It is costly in economic and personal terms when teachers use an approach that will later require "unlearning" and "re-learning".
>
> Learning is enhanced when students have the time to THINK and REFLECT.

Thinking skills can be taught.

> There needs to be a shift in emphasis to learning rather than teaching, with teachers asking themselves what they should do so that their students **learn with understanding.**
>
> Primary school teachers can play a vital role in preparing children to direct and manage their own learning.
>
> Teachers need strategies that take account of the differences in the representations of **novices** and **experts.** Teachers as experts need to be able to **adopt a novice perspective in transmitting knowledge to learners**, and then over time to lead the novices to **construct more expert representations.**
>
> Students respond better when TALKED WITH in two-way communication, rather than being TALKED AT.
>
> Humans are constantly creating their futures. The way to preferred futures is from an understanding of the past and an awareness of the present.
>
> Associationism & behaviourism have little to say about thinking and the nature of knowledge. Piaget and the gestaltists have little to say about instruction.
>
> **(Generally, "behaviourist" objectives in education should be re-stated in "cognitivist" terms.)**

<u>REFERENCES</u>

Botkin J W et al(1979) <u>No Limits To Learning: Bridging the Human Gap</u> A Report of The Club of Rome, Pergamon

Brandwein Paul F(1977) <u>The Reduction of Complexity: Substance, Structure and</u>

Style in Curriculum, International Centre for Educational Advancement, Harcourt Brace Jovanovich

Bruner Jerome S(1973) Beyond the Information Given, George Allen and Unwin

Bruner Jerome S(1960) The Process of Education, Harvard University Press

Capra Fritjof(1983) The Turning Point: Science Society and the Rising Culture, Fontana

Deakin University(1981) Open Campus Programme, ETL 821, The Nature of Teaching and Learning (course materials), Deakin University

Deakin University(1981) Open Campus Programme, ECT 401, Classroom Processes (course materials), Deakin University

Dewey John(1967) Experience and Education, Kappa Delta Pi, Collier Books

Eckersley Richard(1988) Casualties of Change, The predicament of youth in Australia, Commission For the Future, AGPS

Faure Edgar et al(1972) Learning To Be, UNESCO/Harrap

Flavel John H(1977) Cognitive Development, Prentice Hall

Fraenkel Jack(1973) Helping Students Think and Value, Prentice- Hall

Fraenkel Jack(1976) "Agora", Special Fraenkel Edition, Victorian Historical Association, Vol.X No.2

Kant Immanuel(1973) Critique Of Pure Reason (Translated by Norman Kemp), Macmillan

Muller Robert(1985) "A World Core Curriculum", in Future Education, Centre Publications

National Council for Social Studies(1983) Report of the Task Force Into Scope and Sequence

Novak Joseph D(1977) A Theory of Education, Cornell University Press

O'Brien Les B, Hay Trevor C, Tinkler Don E(1984) About Learning: A Proposal For a Seven-Programme Television Series, Report to the National Education Committee of UNICEF Australia Bruntland Report (1987) Our Common Future, World Commission On Environment And Development, O U P

Power Colin(1981) "Introduction to Classroom Processes", in Classroom and Communication, Deakin University Press

Resnick Lauren(1983) "Toward a Cognitive Theory of Instruction", in Learning and Motivation in the Classroom, Erlbaum

Samples Bob(1976) The Metaphoric Mind: A Celebration of Creative Consciousness, Addison-Wesley

Taba Hilda(1966) Teaching Strategies and Cognitive Functioning in Elementary School Children, Cooperative Research Project No. 2404, San Francisco State College

Tinkler Don E(1989) The Humanities Core Curriculum (HCC): An Integrated Curriculum in Social Education for Primary Schools (2nd edn), Macro-View

Tinkler Don(1989) Social Education for Australian Primary Schools, The

Humanities Core Curriculum (HCC): A "Futures" Perspective, Macro-View

Tinkler Don E(1982) "The Rationale, Development, and Application of The Humanities Core Curriculum (HCC)', A Curriculum Alternative for Primary School Social Studies: A Statement on Learning and Teaching in Social Studies K - 6." Unpublished M.Ed.Studies double-project thesis, Monash University

Turner Johanna(1975) Cognitive Development, Methuen

UNESCO(1990) "Report of the International Symposium and Round Table, Qualities Required of Education Today to Meet Foreseeable Demands in the Twenty-First Century", Beijing, People's Republic of China, UNESCO(Distribution: limited)

Vuyk Rita(1981) Overview and Critique of Piaget's Genetic Epistemology 1965 - 1980, Vol.1&2, Academic Press

Vygotsky Lem S(1962) Thought And Language, M.I.T. Press

Wilber Ken(Ed)(1982) The Holographic Paradigm and Other Paradoxes: Exploring the Leading Edge of Science, Shambhala

SOME IMPLICATIONS OF OPEN LEARNING AS CURRICULUM STRATEGY WITHIN FURTHER EDUCATION

By

Stephen D. Reeve

Introduction

As a co-ordinator for Open Learning (OL) within Further Education, it has become increasingly apparent to me that despite the immediate and `hands on' demands of a new approach within a changing environment, time must be taken out to think through the process of open learning on a more theoretical level.

This need exists for a variety of reasons :

As open learning is more readily espoused by Further Education institutions, OL co-ordinators are more and more in the firing line vis-a-vis colleagues and management over educational/training issues

Despite the rapid pace of movement toward open learning (and nationally this is *very* rapid), many staff remain unconvinced or sceptical - they demand far sounder educational arguments than the largely `technical' points often made for OL based on finance, efficiency and staff/student ratios

There may be a tendency for open learning to be adopted primarily for the above technical reasons, regardless of educational debate or the feelings of teaching staff

The *quality* of whatever open learning provision is offered may depend on a comprehension of the theoretical educational basis of the system

Often the educational arguments advanced verge on the tautological, or at least propagandist - as if it should somehow be really obvious that open learning should be better than conventional structures

I will therefore attempt to set out some theoretical landmarks as a rough guide to this territory. I hope this may result in some kind of agreed consensus on how the tenets of Learner-Managed-Learning might influence open learning practice and vice-versa (despite the semantic similarity, the philosophies may not be as similar as might naively be supposed). Although I shall be examining critically the concept of open learning within the curriculum, I should make it plain that I feel a massive amount has already been achieved in `freeing up' the F E curriculum. There are now large numbers of people involved in education or training who without F E flexibility (and particularly open learning) would not have been able to take part. This is a great achievement, but whilst acknowledging this success, my main aim in this chapter is to turn the spotlight onto the use of these techniques within the mainstream curriculum. Here, there is no clear-cut improvement on zero provision, rather an opportunity cost to evaluate, in terms of whether O L techniques provide a better quality learning experience than traditional practice.

As currently fashionable, I will not attempt to define open learning too closely, although a model based on three continua will most effectively demonstrate the flavour of what *open* learning might be.

Fig 16.1 THE THREE CONTINUA MODEL

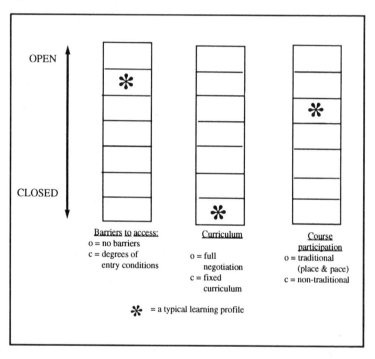

As this model seeks to demonstrate, the three continua represent the most commonly asserted conditions which generally seem to describe the degree of open-ness of the learning which may take place. There is clear scope for incompatibility among the continua - no barriers to entry to a standard course may well be open as far as a college is concerned, albeit undertaken in the college and at a conventional pace. Other colleges may provide courses where the timing and length of study are up to the student but where certain entry criteria remain strong, again such a course might be deemed open. In fact, an institution where `open-ness' exists in any one of the three continua may declare itself to be providing open learning. Critics might suggest that provision could not be said to be open unless the particular continuum(a) considered important to them has a high open-ness score. Thus, some would consider the Open University itself (to many the epitome of good O L practice) as *not* providing open learning because it would score low on the negotiated curriculum scale. The inability of the student to take part in the design and evaluation of the curriculum would demonstrate a closed system. Obviously there would be no debate as to an institution which scored `high' on all three continua, unambiguous open-ness would exist!

The more usual or `softer' consensus however hinges on the issues of access, pace and length of study. This is certainly how most F E institutions view open learning.

As colleges rush headlong into allowing greater flexibility on pace, place and duration, what issues should be addressed to ensure that the system quality is high and that students receive greater benefit than within conventional practice ?

Educational Philosophy

The philosophy behind open learning is worth exploring and may reveal potential problems and contradictions. The work of Boot and Hodgson (Hodgson, Mann, Snell. eds.1987) is very illuminating here and highlights a possible major discrepancy between the often stated aims of open learning, and the technique's means of achieving them. At issue here is whether the aims of *independent study* have been `stolen' by open learning and are incompatible with the technique used in O L. Such a discrepancy depends on the interpretation of the idea of control - as to whether control of the pace and place of an externally organised programme could lead to self-development in the same way as control of the independent learning experience. Thus, there is great emphasis in much of the O L literature on giving control and allowing self-development to the student (traditionally `independent' aims) whereas in fact the control may be somewhat superficial and the self-development limited by the nature of the externally structured learning programme. Interpretation of what constitutes *real* control is open to much discussion, and is perhaps only the latest manifestation of the long running `nature versus nurture' debate. Boot and Hodgson draw a distinction between a *disseminationist* and a *developmental* philosophy, and it does not take too much research to discover that most open learning is firmly based on the dissemination model.

There are important implications here - dissemination assumes that `knowledge' may be parcelled up into carefully weighed chunks and `delivered', largely by carefully pre-written materials in a serial form, within an externally designed and assessed curriculum context. The student receives and internalises this content.

There is much here that runs contrary to the tenets of the *independent study* school of thought, where student responsibility for curriculum, tutor/student negotiation, experiential, non-serial learning and spontanaiety are essential. Developmentalists would argue that meaningful learning could not easily occur within a dissemination/ reception based system.

The developmental versus dissemination debate may well seem rather abstract to teachers actually getting on with the job, but it might have a profound effect on their methods as open learning becomes more widespread. This difference between philosophies may lead a progressive teacher to champion the cause of open learning as a way to encourage <u>independent</u> learners, little realising that the system may be far more constricting, alienating and non-developmental than a well taught conventional course. It is as well that such issues are examined, because the aims of independent (in its strong sense) and open learning may not co-incide. When this is understood, a decision to follow one path or the other, or more importantly to comprehend the difference and adjust accordingly, may be made.

Once a deliberate effort is made to come to terms with such issues, it becomes immediately apparent that more depth of analysis is needed, and one finds oneself swimming (or sinking?) in the murky waters of learning theory itself...

What is, and how do you achieve successful open learning?

In order to talk about good or successful open learning, it is useful to come to terms with what makes for good learning generally. A great deal of progress has been made in this area, and illuminative field research and educational psychology have been welded into a generally agreed consensus. There is no space here to explore these issues in depth, so I intend to highlight certain areas which I feel have most to offer in terms of good open learning practice.

Possible Consensus

Following on from the pioneering work of Marton and Saljo (1976), much work has been done to explain and categorise 'successful' learning. Much of the consensus centres on the idea of differing approaches by individuals' to learning. Starting from the basic differentiation (Marton and Saljo) between "deep" and "surface" learners, contributors to the debate have identified several other factors which impinge on learning - intrinsic/extrinsic approaches, environmental context, strategic/non-strategic awareness, hidden curricula, and degrees of self-awareness of learning.

Such factors, by and large, may be incorporated into the famous Entwistle (1983, revised 1988) four dimensional matrix. Although an abstract model, certain highly pragmatic features may be gleaned which may be of direct use for the improvement of any student's learning ability. It seems clear that an intrinsically motivated, holist-minded, strategically aware individual will learn most effectively. This may simply sound like common sense, but how many teaching programmes explicitly aim to ease a student towards such a set of approaches, rather than fill him/her with a set of data and skills deemed appropriate for a given curriculum?

On the other hand, the least effective learner may be familiar to many teachers - no or low levels of motivation (intrinsically or extrinsically), serialist but confused in approach, non-strategically aware of how to succeed within a given environment.

This approach theory may be of particular importance to colleges moving over to large scale curriculum coverage by open learning, because there is far more responsibility placed on the individual for their own learning. When working at one's own pace becomes the norm, there will be a tendency for a class to 'atomise'; students will lose the familiarity of set conditions (particularly the 'solidarity' of formally proceeding at the same rate) and the key to individual success will be far more approach-dependent. With class 'equality' of pace and content gone, the individual student will be shown up far more clearly by his/her approach to learning and indeed *ability to learn*.

This is where I feel educational theory has most to offer, and may provide the common ground for the concepts of learner-managed-learning and successful flexible learning practice. If individuality is to be the key to future mainstream further education provision, then colleges must provide students with help as to how to become <u>good individual learners</u>. The lessons from theory must be understood, and the one which could be the key to an approaches-based methodology is the notion of consciousness or self-awareness of learning, - or in the slightly more mystical jargon, the idea of "meta-learning".

Meta-learning

Here, I feel, is a concept where all sides begin to converge - the predictions of approaches theory, the experience of the independent study movement, the anecdotal evidence of the teaching profession and the claimed benefits of open or flexible learning. Meta-learning is the process of metaphorically `standing back' from direct learning which may be going on, and examining and questioning the relationship between self and the processes involved in that learning.

Encouraging students to become cogniscent, or consciously aware of, and responsible for, their own learning is going to be one of the main challenges for open or flexible learning. It may well be that the new techniques will demand that teachers spend a great deal of their time helping students to arrive at the `meta' state. Pre-written packages and multi-media information systems will provide the content, but to pick effectively from these products and achieve successful learning, students will need to be taught how to be wise consumers. There is a lurking danger that open learning packages may be handed out en-masse (albeit backed-up by `workshops') to a student body not geared up to study from such materials consciously or effectively.

As the ideas of open learning gain currency, there seems to be an assumption that *of itself* the technique will somehow lead students to become self-aware learners. This could be a very large educational mistake, and at worst lead to large numbers of isolated young people floundering within a system where under conventional techniques they may have acquitted themselves well.

If then, open learning is to have increased emphasis, it is incumbent upon colleges to develop techniques which will provide students with the wherewithal to flourish under these new conditions. This is easy to say, but perhaps harder to put into practice on the large scale.

The work of Biggs (1985) in Australia has shown that techniques can certainly be used to attempt to change or re-orientate student approaches towards the pre-conditions for more successful learning outcomes.

I would propose a possible curriculum structure at policy level which may enable colleges to equip their students for survival and success within this new environment. Drawing upon the tenets of the independent study movement as the most useful way to approach the instigation or enhancement of meta-learning, and adapting the curriculum model of Professor Eraut(1976) would, I suggest, provide a sensible methodology.

Eraut's curriculum model is an extremely useful way to view a given curriculum, and in figure 16.2 is set out in conventional mode.

Using the same structure, Eraut has also modelled the independent study curriculum (fig.16.3.) with its obviously very different ethos.

Figure 16.2 ERAUT'S CURRICULUM MODEL

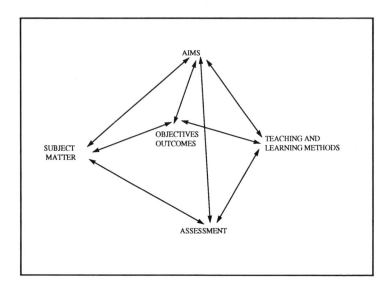

Figure 16.3 MODIFIED ERAUT CURRICULUM MODEL

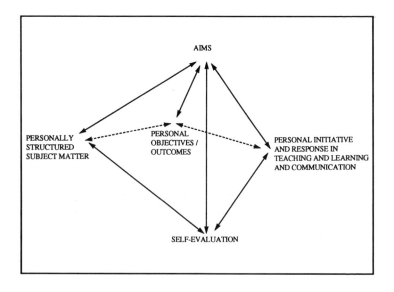

Whilst acknowledging that fig.16.3. is probably inappropriate to all but the most progressive of further education establishments, I suggest that an adapted model, sitting somewhere between the two, might be an appropriate tool for F.E. curriculum managers (fig.16.4)

In such a model, the need to promote `meta-learning', self-responsibility and critical awarenesss has been explicitly recognised, even though the model does not espouse the more `extreme' forms of negotiated curriculum independence. If the acknowledgement and engendering of this concept forms the bedrock of flexible learning policy, it may allow colleges to prepare their students for successful flexible learning via awareness of what they are doing and why, albeit within a largely externally set curriculum. This seems to me to lay firm foundations at a curriculum planning level, rather than simply hoping or assuming that the `magic' of open learning will solve all sorts of educational and financial problems.

Figure 16.4 ADAPTED ERAUT CURRICULUM MODEL

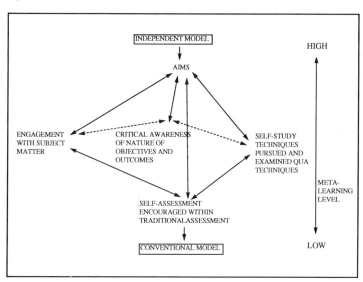

Thus, in such a model, the student would become more engaged, (perhaps *really* empowered), rather than being told they've been empowered) in all four areas :

The comprehension of objectives and certification would be encouraged at both a critically evaluative (intrinsic), and a strategically aware (extrinsic) level

The student should become aware of self-study as a technique, not just `do it', which may lead on to greater satisfaction and levels of critical analysis

Although externally set assessment will be most typical, students will be encouraged towards conscious self-assessment, and tutor assessment would incorporate this increased level of awareness

The student should become more engaged with subject matter at best because of self-confidence gained through more real control, or more simply as a by-product of greater strategic awareness

As Biggs has put it at its most simple, " if students can perceive what they want and how to get it, and they want it sufficiently, then it is likely that the students concerned could indeed become better learners." This is the message which those involved with open learning should carry to their institutions - it is not just a case of teaching differently to the same students, but of helping the students to become different in order to cope effectively with the new techniques.

In short, what is at issue here, is whether colleges will be able to equip their students to undertake *learner-managed-learning* or *self-managed programme pursuit.* There could be a chasm of difference between the two for all concerned, colleges, teachers and students.

Although there has been stress within this chapter on theoretical issues, I hope to explore the many day-to-day problems of open learning, leading toward recognition of how the theoretical might inform and indeed even solve some of these problems.

REFERENCES

Biggs J B (1985) Metalearning and Study Processes, British Journal of Educational Psychology,pp 190-211

Entwistle N and Waterston S (1988) Approaches to Studying and Levels of Processing in University Students, British Journal of Educational Psychology, 58pp 258-266

Eraut M (1976) Should Curriculum Decisions be made `for' or `by' the Independent Learner, Conference Paper for the C D F H E programme, University of Sussex

Hodgson V, Mann S, Snell R (Eds)(1987), Beyond Distance Teaching- Towards Open Learning, Open University Press

Morton F and Saljo R (1976) Symposium: Learning Processes and Strategies - II, on Qualitative Differences in Learning - II, Outcome as a Function if the Learner's conception of the Task, British Journal of Educational Psychology, 46, 115-127

SECTION C:
POLICY ISSUES

CHAPTER 17

BRINGING SELF-DIRECTED LEARNING INTO THE MAINSTREAM OF TERTIARY EDUCATION

By

David Boud and Joy Higgs

Introduction

It is a part of the rhetoric of higher education institutions that we should be producing graduates capable of, and wishing to pursue, lifelong learning. Nobody would dispute this as a desirable goal, but there is often a considerable gap between what is desired and what is likely to be achieved. With a goal like this it is difficult to recognise the extent to which it is pursued because it is subject to a variety of interpretations. If we could easily operationalise it, we could pursue it more readily. Frequently in our curricula such goals are identified and some attention is paid to achieving them through the promotion of independent or self-directed learning. This may occur through a variety of activities: project work, laboratory enquiry activities, learning contracts and other forms of negotiated learning and open-ended assignments. The degree of emphasis on self-directed learning may vary in each of these strategies, but they represent in general a shift towards students taking greater responsibility for, and a more active role in, the teaching and learning process.

Despite the interest which has been generated in self-directed learning, and the increasingly successful implementation of associated methods, it too often remains a supplement to the curriculum, designed to enhance it, rather than a fundamental basis for curriculum design and/or implementation. For instance, an emphasis on self-directed learning may be restricted to one unit of a course in which students pursue a learning contract (Knowles, 1975). It can also represent a negation of teacher responsibility as much as an attempt to foster student activity when staff withdraw completely and let the students get on with projects or assignments entirely unaided. Containing self-directed learning to a specific part of a course can lead to the negative effect that students only associate the goal of self-direction with one content area or as the prelude to graduation. This does not necessarily achieve the intended effect of promoting the development of self-directed learning skills which students apply throughout their learning activities and adopt once they leave the higher education system.

In some cases self-directed learning may appear in a general goal statement, such as "the promotion of learner independence", in a curriculum document. However, the day-to-day reality for students, particularly those in professional and vocational courses, is that throughout many of their years of study they must follow the detailed path set by their teachers, in the manner which these teachers require, and they must conform to the assessment tasks which these teachers and/or external authorities set.

The aim of this paper is to discuss issues associated with applying the goals and methods associated with self-directed learning across the curriculum. This will be referred to as mainstreaming of self-directed learning. We are suggesting that educators should consider taking self-direction from the periphery of curricula, from being the exception to the norm, and making it a central aspect. Such a shift has many implications and there are some dilemmas to be faced if it is to be attempted. It would involve relinquishing self-directed learning as a particular strategy which can be easily labelled and identified in certain parts of the curriculum. It would then become a normal part of the content and process of learning programmes. This task is a challenge to be confronted afresh in each particular institution and programme, with each programme carrying its own unique problems to be addressed.

What is self-directed learning and why might it be used?

We take self-directed learning to be an approach to learning in which the behaviour of the learner is characterised by:

1)   responsibility for and critical awareness of, his or her own learning process and outcome,

2)   a high level of self-direction in performing learning activities and solving problems which are associated with the learning task,

3)   active input to decision-making regarding the learning task, and

4)   the use of teachers as a resource persons (Higgs, 1988).

There are two other aspects of the nature of self-directed learning programmes which we wish to emphasise. The first of these is that learner self-direction does not mean learning in isolation. Rather it connotes internal motivation and the impetus for learning coming from within the learner. Learners may elect to learn by themselves. However, many authors argue strongly that effective learning involves interalia interaction with others. Griffith (1987), for instance, discusses the concept of independence versus interdependence in learning programmes. She stresses the importance of learners valuing the contributions each can make to the other's learning. Similarly, Heron (1989) argues that learners can only be self-directing in reciprocal relations with other self-directed persons.

Secondly, self-directed learning can take many different forms within which a number of phases and a variety of learner behaviours occur. It cannot be identified with any single activity or set of behaviours on the part of learners. This has been illustrated by the work of Taylor (1987). She studied in depth a group of postgraduate education students working together in a subject which involved them in making many of the decisions about the direction of process of study. She identified four phases (disorientation, exploration, reorientation, equilibrium) and phase transitions (disconfirmation, naming the problem, reflection, sharing the discovery) which occurred in the group. Self-direction in learning is widely acknowledged as being a fundamental educational goal. It is central within an important class of goals related to the process of and responsibilities for learning and it contributes to other goals such as growth in ability to learn and ability to apply learning to all aspects of work and living in society (Boud 1988). Harris (1989, p.112) regards the aim of self-directed learning as being:

"to assist individuals to take increasing control over their learning processes and content. In this way, they will develop the realization that they have the power to alter their individual and social environment and to create their own reality. This is the 'empowerment view' of ... education".

Self-directed learning as defined above closely parallels the goals of most courses leading to professional status. In particular, the goals of these courses include the fostering of: independent learning skills, the ability to engage effectively in problem solving and decision making in autonomous and group situations, the pursuit of lifelong learning and the ability to deal constructively with an expanding knowledge base.

The concept of the lifelong learner and the promotion of lifelong learning is central to the theory and practice of self-directed learning. Knowles (1970), for instance, identified the main characteristics of self-directed learners as being: an increasing self-directedness, a readiness to learn in relation to life tasks and roles, a rich background of experience that serves as a resource for learning and an orientation to learning which is problem-centred rather than subject-centred.

Within professional education the importance of self-directed learning skills such as the ability to effectively reflect on and modify their approaches to learning is well-recognised. A powerful argument is presented by Schon (1987) who addresses the dilemma of preparing students for the demands of professional practice. He asks "can the prevailing concepts of professional education ever yield a curriculum adequate to the complex, unstable, uncertain, and conflictual worlds of practice?" (p.12). In common with many educators, Schon (1987) argues that students cannot be taught what they need to know. Instead, he believes learning can be assisted by "coaches". Related ideas were developed by Rogers (1969) who introduced the notion of teachers as facilitators of learning, and by Candy (1988a) who emphasised the learner as the focus of learning programmes by referring to the learner and his/her "assistants".

One of the ultimate goals of fostering the development of the skills of self-directed learning such as reflection, is to promote their transfer into life and work situations. Boud, Keogh and Walker (1985, p.19) describe reflection as one of the keys to effective decision making. They concluded from a study of the role of reflection in learning that "it is only when we bring our ideas to our consciousness (i.e. reflection) that we can evaluate them and begin to make choices about what we will and will not do". The importance of reflection in self-directed learning is stressed by Harris (1989) and also by Brookfield (1986) who regards reflection as an integral part of the self-directed learner's pursuit of meaning. That is, encouraging the pursuit of meaning and the ability to make reasoned decisions in the learning environment is the first step to promoting the application of these to the student's professional role.

In the context of professional practice we often speak of the concept of professional autonomy. This term connotes independence in decision making and action, taking responsibility for one's actions and the demand for accountability towards those who receive the services of the professional. Self-directed learning by its very nature encourages each of these three factors. Candy (1988b) argues that the development of autonomy also includes subject matter autonomy. This involves the ability to make judgements, to determine one's own viewpoint and to be able to defend one's position in a given knowledge area. Such subject matter autonomy is vital to today's professionals.

Professional autonomy brings with it accountability. In the classroom we see this as the student taking responsibility for his/her own learning. In fieldwork settings the student or graduate must take responsibility for his/her professional decisions and actions. Learning programmes which involve high levels of unilateral decision making and responsibility by teachers, promote learner passivity and dependence. By comparison, programmes which emphasise adult learning, promote learners taking responsibility for their own learning. Tompkins and McGraw (1988) report on the success of negotiated learning contracts in nursing education in the promotion of independent behaviours, cognitive achievement and autonomous learning. The School for Independent Study at the University of East London had been in operation for over fifteen years (Stephenson, 1988) (See Chapter 2). In programmes at this School (which cover a very wide range of disciplines), independent learning was at the centre of each student's learning. These programmes involve risk for the students. They require them to take responsibility for their learning and actions over periods of up to three years While few students enter these programmes with such abilities, most of them were found to develop the capacity to meet the independent learning demands of the programme and achieve high levels of performance.

Professionals need to develop reasoning and problem solving skills which can be applied to their work role. A number of innovative curricula such as the problem-based learning medical programmes at Newcastle University, Australia and McMaster University, Canada have been created around the goal of developing these skills (Boud and Feletti, 1991). Such programmes include teaching and learning strategies which foster the development of the ability to reason and solve problems effectively. These strategies emphasise allowing students to explore, to take risks, to reflect on their thoughts and actions, to experiment and discuss their thoughts and experiences with others. The McMaster programme, for instance, requires students to direct their own learning in a way that is compatible with the learning objectives of their learning group. National examination results have found McMaster students to be above average in their problem solving ability (Ferrier, Marrin and Seidman, 1988).

Why mainstreaming?

There are three main responses to why we should wish to mainstream self-directed learning approaches. Firstly, the inclusion of self-directed learning in curricula can help students develop the skills and attitudes needed for their professional work role (e.g. lifelong learning skills). Secondly, research in education has identified a strong link between the context of learning at curriculum level and the approaches to learning adopted by students. Thirdly, isolated classes or courses in self-directed learning (as will be discussed below) are not likely to be as effective as a more total curriculum self-directed learning approach (i.e. mainstreaming).

Redesigning curricula can be a time consuming and costly exercise. This is particularly so where changes to curricula are associated with discarding previous programmes or materials which were expensive to develop (in time or money) or where innovations proposed are costly. For instance, the introduction of curricula based largely on self-directed learning principles and strategies may require additional staff or add to existing staff workload. It may also result in more efficient use of staff time or lower unit costs. Stephenson (1988), for example, reports that the programmes in the School of Independent Study ran at a lower cost than that of other programmes in the same institution. We argue that self-directed learning can be implemented in some form or other no matter what the restrictions on resources: it can be made to work at whatever resource level is available. Whether the outcomes are as equally beneficial is impossible to say at present.

Curriculum developers considering the implementation of a mainstreaming approach to self-directed learning need to answer two pertinent questions. What benefits could be gained and are these worth the cost? What problems could arise and can these be dealt with effectively? We believe that the potential benefits of this strategy outweigh problems which may arise and that knowledgeable planning and implementation of the strategy can avert or manage such problems.

The value of self-directed learning is strongly supported by the findings of a large body of educational research conducted in the area of promoting effective student learning (Biggs, 1982; Entwistle, 1981; Pask, 1976; Perry, 1970). This research has identified different approaches students have to learning and the effects of learning contexts on these learning approaches.

An important focus of this research has been on the differences between deep (or meaningful) approaches to learning and surface (or rote) approaches, and on factors within the learning environment which promote each approach. According to Ramsden (1988):

"Deep approaches exemplify the type of learning that employers and teachers expect students to demonstrate. Only through using these approaches can students gain mastery of concepts and a firm hold on detailed factual knowledge in a given subject area. Such approaches embody the imaginative and adaptive skills and wide sphere of interests that are increasingly demanded in the world of work. In acute contrast surface approaches epitomize low-quality learning, are geared to short-term requirements, and focus on the need faithfully to reproduce fragments of information presented in class or textbooks. ... surface approaches are concerned with 'getting the right answer' to the exclusion of knowing how to get it and of what it means when it has been obtained" (p.20).

In landmark research in this area, Entwistle and Ramsden (1983) found that tertiary students' approaches to learning were influenced by the context in which they were studying. They found that deep approaches occurred most often in contexts characterised by freedom in learning, less formality, good teaching input, a good social climate and clear goals. By comparison surface or rote learning approaches are more likely to occur where there are heavy workloads.

The link between student learning behaviour and the learning environment has also been demonstrated at the University of Auckland (Jones and Putterill, 1988; Jones, Caird and Putterill, 1989). In reviewing these research findings, Jones (1990) reported that attempts to improve teaching/learning practices within individual courses generally met with limited success. He argued that educators need to challenge the educational theories and practices which influence the total curriculum. This is an argument in favour of mainstreaming rather than isolating self-directed learning within curricula.

"Teaching in its broadest sense defines the framework within which learning occurs" (Wilson, 1981, p.15). Given this viewpoint the role of teachers is to promote learning by providing such a framework. If educators wish to facilitate the development of learner self-direction, reflection, subject matter autonomy, problem solving skills and a commitment to lifelong learning, then a positive step would be to incorporate self-directed learning into the total curricula.

To succeed, educational innovations must fit within the constraints and constructs of educational institutions sufficiently well for them to be sustained by typical teachers without heroic effort. They need to be applied widely and become part of normal practice. Mainstreaming of self-directed learning has the potential to achieve this success.

An analogy can be drawn between mainstreaming self-directed learning and the place of communication and study skills in the curriculum. Programmes aiming to teach such skills are widespread (Gibbs, 1981; Novak and Gowin, 1984; Smith, 1983). Communication and study skills are being increasingly incorporated as integral parts of all tertiary courses, not just adjuncts to be given special treatment by special staff. This situation has occurred because evidence suggests that separate study skills courses have limited effectiveness (Biggs, 1986; Martin and Ramsden, 1986). Firstly, it has been recognised that it is inadequate and incongruent for specific teachers to conduct courses related to the fundamental aspects of studying and using a body of knowledge, in a manner and time which is separate from the main activities of the course. Secondly, it has been realised that it is inefficient and ineffective to have activities which require an additional step to integrate them into other subjects or programmes.

During the transitional period of this trend in higher education, when the importance of study skills and communication was not fully accepted by subject teachers and when new populations of students unfamiliar with higher education were arriving, it was probably necessary for these skills to be given particular emphasis. However, for the most part, the marginalising of these activities which occurred should now be regarded as a sign of ineffectiveness. Educators are in a position to learn from this experience with study skills and, recognising the fundamental nature of learner self-direction, to place this approach to learning where it belongs, at the core of the curriculum.

Mainstreaming self-directed learning: implementation

In advocating mainstreaming, we acknowledge that there can be variation in the extent to which self-directed learning is a dominant feature of the teaching and learning process of courses. Therefore, courses pursuing self-directed learning may appear to be very different. For instance, they may range from problem-based learning activities, to learning projects or individual learning contracts. The common elements of the various modes of self-directed learning programmes are:

1)   a focus on learner independence and responsibility within a given learning context,

2)   an emphasis on student involvement in decision-making about both content and process, and

3)   a concern about learning how to learn and learning about learning, not just what is learned.

The manner of implementation of mainstreaming can vary. In a more global sense mainstreaming could involve a complete reappraisal of all aspects of the curriculum to introduce self-directed learning as the organising principle for an entire programme of study. Alternatively (or in addition) a syllabus emphasising self-directed learning might move away from conventional subjects and focus on student competencies, with lectures used only in a very limited way and assessment being mostly negotiated. In a more subtle manner, mainstreaming could involve the adoption of new independent learning goals for all components of a course and a revision of these components at the discretion of the teachers involved so that these goals are pursued as part of all subjects, but not in a standardised manner.

Adopting mainstreaming is not always the best strategy for those who wish to promote the goals of self-directed learning. It should only occur once the teaching/learning practices which are being considered are sufficiently robust and mature to be used by both supporters and those less enthusiastic about this strategy. Deciding if and when to mainstream is a decision which needs to be well considered. Research conducted by Tompkins and McGraw (1988) in nursing education found that dependent learners experienced frustration and anxiety when first introduced to programmes focussing on self-directed learning. However, their study found that experience with self-directed learning can improve the learners' independence and can become highly satisfying to learners.

Dealing with implementation dilemmas

Dilemma 1: Who controls self-directed learning?

Self-directed learning has in its very name an implication that students have control over their courses. This can contribute to confusion and misunderstanding in educational institutions where the assumption is that teachers are in control of the educational process. It can also lead to fears on the part of teachers that they may introduce a process which is going to undermine their professional standing and make life very difficult for them.

This is based on a misconception about the practice of self-directed learning. Within educational systems as they are presently constructed, it is not conceivable to have students exercising complete self-directedness all the time in all aspects of their life as students. Such activity is not necessary to achieve the goal of producing people who are self-directed as learners. What is desirable is that sufficient experience of self-direction occurs throughout the course for students to regard this both as a responsibility and skill to be acquired and an opportunity to be enjoyed.

The goal is to build into courses some self-direction from the start, preferably increasing in amount as the students grow in their ability to use a self-directed learning approach. This strategy has analogies in other areas such as the development of critical thought and written expression skills. Moving students towards these skills progressively is not inconsistent with the achievement of other conventional learning outcomes criteria such as knowledge of content or exercise of skills.

The question which educators need to address is how much independence do learners need and want? Candy (1987) discusses this point in some detail. He cites many studies (e.g Brookfield, 1982; Tough, 1978, 1979) which have demonstrated that the majority of adults engage in independent learning activities outside educational institutions. However, he argues, there is also substantial research that many adults have a limited desire or ability to be self-directed and seek or rely on direction or external control (Entwistle et al, 1979; Parlett, 1970; Rogers, 1969; Witkin et al, 1977). Candy (1987, p.174) concludes that the willingness of learners "to accept increased control will depend on whether or not, in any particular case, they judge it to be a valid strategy and a situation from which they can learn". In promoting an increase in learning control and responsibility therefore, teachers need to ensure that students are able to see the relevance and effectiveness of self-directed learning approaches.

Another important factor in independent learning contexts is the extent to which learners are prepared (e.g. through past or current educational programmes) for the demands and benefits of self-directed learning. The concept of "learner task maturity" (Higgs, 1989) is pertinent here. It refers to the extent to which students have learning skills and experience of previous tasks which enables them to effectively and independently engage in the learning task at hand. The level of the learner's "task maturity" therefore, is an important consideration when determining the level of independence to expect of the learner and the extent to which the teacher needs to prepare the learner for the self-direction demands of the learning programme.

Griffith (1987), in discussing the issue of authority and power in education, argues for interdependence. Her substantial research and teaching experience at the Ontario Institute for Studies in Education in Toronto have led her to the conclusion that both dependent and independent learning situations are limited. Dependent learners are guided by external criteria while independent learners are more inner directed. She argues that in interdependent learning, power becomes a more positive factor, i.e. empowerment of oneself and others, rather than being under the control of another (dependency) or striving for self-control (independence). Interdependence is the nature of the control balance that "self-directed learning" programmes are seeking to achieve with their emphasis on learning with and through others. At this point we can see that the term "self-directed learning programmes" is somewhat misleading. What we are presenting is the picture of learning programmes where learner self-direction and responsibility are key elements, but where other learners, teachers and resource people play interactive roles.

Dilemma 2: Finding an appropriate curriculum framework

The traditional discipline-centred framework for a degree or diploma programme is excellent at promoting a subject-centred orientation to learning, but it can act as a substantial inhibitor in the pursuit of goals which cut across subject boundaries.

This is as true for professional goals such as the promotion of self-direction. Students need to be able to exercise self-directedness both within subject areas and across subject areas.

While subject-matter autonomy (Candy, 1988b) is an important aspect of self-directedness, the subject-centred view of the curriculum is not the only one, and some of the most substantial progress towards self-directed learning is being made within other frameworks. Approaches to the curriculum which involve the planned development of competencies is one, organising the curriculum around a selection of vocationally oriented problems is another. Whichever alternative is chosen, it is necessary to engage in an analysis of the structure of knowledge in the field being examined, and the creation of frameworks for the development of an understanding of this knowledge. Such frameworks would need to be appropriate for the discipline being studied, they would need to be readily appreciated by students and staff and they would include a set of educational principles and strategies which were compatible with the programme's goals and context.

An example of such a framework can be found in the reconceptualisation of the curriculum which took place at the University of Western Sydney, Hawkesbury in the Faculty of Agriculture (Bawden, 1985). Here, staff decided to explore what constituted the field of agricultural education and what was the role of an agriculturalist within this field. This led to a portrayal of the domain of agriculture and the development of a set of broad competencies which provide the framework for the course. The staff determined that their courses should aim to produce agriculturalists who take a systems and situation-improving perspective rather than graduates who possess the specialist component skills which are found in agricultural research and in parts of the industry.

Cornwall (1988, p.246) provides a set of general features of a structure or framework for independent learning:

1)   clearly defined goals.

2)   availability of the necessary material and human resources.

3)   an understanding of the roles and responsibilities of both the teacher and the students.

4)   arrangements by which both parties can be prepared for the new demands to be imposed on them and can acquire some of the appropriate skills in a 'fail-safe' way.

5)   means by which the success of the course can be checked as it proceeds and if necessary changes without bureaucratic snags.

As well as having desirable elements within the curriculum framework, there needs to be congruence between these elements. Particularly when employing "whole curriculum" or mainstreaming strategies it is important to achieve consistency between the messages students receive through stated goals, learning activities and assessment. Students' perceptions of these messages and of conflicts between them can result in them adopting learning behaviours contrary to those intended by the teachers. Therefore, part of the teacher's role in introducing an innovative learning approach is to re-educate students conceptions of learning (Eizenberg, 1986).

Dilemma 3:   Establishing a suitable institutional context for self-directed learning

The task of embedding any innovation into an institution or department has two aspects.   Firstly, it is necessary to gain institutional approval and support and to create within the institution a context of active pursuit of this innovation and its goals.   This requires the commitment of colleagues and academic managers who might not be directly involved in teaching.   The second essential step is to create a context which is conducive to this innovative type of learning within the overall context of the course.   This requires taking a student-centred viewpoint in order to examine how students are likely to experience the educational process.

Good ideas may fail when their proponents assume that rational argument is all that is necessary for acceptance.   Presentation of a good case does not guarantee acceptance, nor is it all that is required to develop the necessary staff commitment which is essential if the ideas are to be carried through to implementation. Attention needs to be given to the process of introducing change in education (e.g. Fullan, 1982, Havelock, 1973).

Of particular importance is increasing the flexibility of the written or unwritten rules which govern educational programmes within the given institution.   For example, innovative educational approaches such as self-directed learning, may have a far greater chance of success if barriers such as the following were removed or lessened: one hour timetable slots, the form and deadlines for assignments, and standardised lecture/tutorial patterns.   These apparently administrative changes can be profoundly liberating for student learning, and can improve the chance of success of innovative teaching/learning strategies.

Another consideration is that of taking account of the interests and concerns of colleagues and responding to them.   Self-directed learning can potentially be disruptive to other teachers in the system when it is not widespread.   It is not a good strategy to alienate colleagues by having students regularly putting in more work on your course to the detriment of their work in others.   Neither is it desirable for students' work in your course to suffer because assessment pressures in other subjects absorbs much of students' out-of-class energies and time.

Gaining commitment to change in educational institutions is a substantial undertaking which requires careful planning and involvement of colleagues in working through the problems and issues which are likely to arise.   The thought that self-directed learning can be instituted through a decision determined at a single point of time is unrealistic.   Colleagues will not be supportive and will not have the necessary stake in the outcomes unless they have had the opportunity to explore proposed changes and be part of the decision making process.

Dilemma 4:   Ensuring content goals are dealt with effectively

A major concern within higher education for the professions is that relevant areas to be covered should be carefully defined.   Much effort is expended upon identifying and proportioning course content so that these goals are allocated to various subjects.   However, insufficient attention is often given to how the content ought to be presented and learned.   Frequently, learning strategies which involve student choice in content or process are regarded as inappropriate or undesirable since they can result in students learning different content or failing to "cover the content".

For this reason self-directed learning as a teaching/learning strategy is often seen as being only suitable for elective subjects or for subjects where dealing with specific aspects of content is less important.

Students need not only to develop self-directed learning skills to cope with their existing learning requirements, they also need them to cope with the increasing knowledge base in their professions. Curriculum developers and teachers need to achieve a satisfactory compromise between these two goals. Graduating practitioners in whatever field need not only to demonstrate satisfactory "beginning practitioner" competence but also to develop this competence throughout their working careers and to have the capacity to respond appropriately to changing needs of the community. Mainstreaming self-directed learning as part of the overall curriculum teaching/learning strategies not only develops this lifelong learning capacity, but it is compatible with the achievement of entry-level competence. That is, this approach is an investment in future learning as well as in current effectiveness. The successful combination of independence in learning and "content coverage" has been demonstrated in numerous vocational programmes (Ferrier et al, 1988; Tompkins and McGraw, 1988).

Mainstreaming self-directed learning does not remove the role of the teacher as "guardian of the discipline". Teachers do have the responsibility to protect our intellectual heritage and pass it on to others. However, they are not the only sources of knowledge, and they do not need to retain the position of "knowledge-givers". Instead, teachers need to become guardians of their discipline in a more profound sense. They can help students to learn effectively by providing ready entry points into knowledge, maps for the newcomer and the intermediate learner, and feedback on the processes and outcomes of learning. They can also contribute greatly to the resources which learners draw upon. Teachers may need to direct more of their attention to the design and structuring of learning activities and support materials, and less to the verbal presentation of information. This is a new role for many and there is an important role for staff development in preparing the ground for this.

The challenge which teachers and programme designers face is to incorporate both guidance and choice into the learning programme. This needs to be done in such a way that justice is done to the discipline, the whole student group and individual students. Also, the teacher needs to work within existing time, feasibility and accreditation constraints, while at the same time pursuing the goal of helping students to learn how-to-learn. Some examples of strategies which can be used to cope with various aspects of this prescription include:

1)   building enquiry activities into the curriculum in a carefully staged manner to encourage the systematic acquisition of the investigative skills which are closely related to learning how-to-learn. Students progressively become capable of undertaking enquiries where they have to make most of the decisions for themselves (e.g. Boud, Dunn and Hegarty-Hazel, 1986);

2)   documenting students' existing (entry) learning and allowing flexibility in course design for student input to content

choices (for instance by the selection of topic areas to be dealt with in a course, based on individual students' learning needs, interests or abilities).

Dilemma 5: Developing appropriate forms of student assessment

Formal study in a learning institution brings with it the requirement of assessment to accredit the student's performance. This is particularly important in vocational courses where government registration boards regulate standards of professional entry and performance. Also, it is becoming widely accepted that assessment influences and even determines what and how students learn (Elton, 1982; Newble and Jaeger, 1983; Rowntree, 1977). Studies by Marton and Saljo (1976) and Ramsden (1984) have demonstrated that assessment methods can profoundly influence students' approach to learning, in particular their use of deep and surface approaches to learning.

Assessment should reflect the range of goals of a learning programme, including the promotion of independent learning skills, i.e. these should be assessed along with any other core learning goals. Self-direction in learning implies an emphasis on self-assessment of learning needs and outcomes (Boud, 1991). Assessment strategies should not undermine the pursuit of self-direction in learning.

There is an apparent contradiction in the idea of teacher assessment of (students') self-directed learning. In relation to formative assessment this problem is fairly easily dealt with. We have already identified the teacher's role as a guide to students' learning. Teachers also act as resource people in self-directed learning situations. Therefore informal assessment and feedback on students' performance, whether sought or unsought by the learner, is not incompatible with self-directed learning in formal courses. It guides learning, encourages student performance and serves as a comparison for the student's self-assessment.

Summative assessment is potentially more problematic. The question which needs to be addressed is: can teachers fulfil institutional demands for assessment of student performance and also foster self-direction in learning including self-assessment? Issues concerning the use of self-assessment in student grading are discussed in detail elsewhere (Boud, 1989). The studies reported in this paper suggest that the demands of summative assessment do not need to undermine an emphasis on self-assessment. However, the role and process of self-assessment needs to be carefully considered and overall assessment practices should be designed to ensure that students' self-assessment does not serve, intentionally or unintentionally, to fool themselves or others. Self-assessment which is unmoderated or conducted in isolation from clear criteria or from other people is not appropriate in institutional settings.

Where self-directed learning is a major element of the teaching/learning process, it is necessary to involve students in decision making about assessment. For instance, students could determine the criteria and process of a self or peer assessment exercise and implement the agreed procedure. To satisfy the external or institutional demands of accreditation, such procedures could be monitored or moderated by teachers, for instance, with the teacher using the same assessment tool and negotiating with students the final grade where significant discrepancies occurred between the student and teacher marks. Alternatively, students could engage in one of the collaborative assessment strategies as proposed by Heron (1988) or develop a self-assessed profile of their learning achievements which is validated by staff (for example, Boud, 1992).

Getting started

The challenge of mainstreaming is a substantial one and anyone contemplating this task will need to find persuasive responses to the dilemmas we have posed. We have provided examples of strategies which have been used in different kinds of institution.

Getting started does require a substantial commitment and in many places it may well be necessary to introduce more of the elements of self-directed learning into existing subjects and to introduce staff to the potential and implementation of self-directed learning before mainstreaming is contemplated. A momentum of interest needs to be generated as the ideas build and spread to other areas.

It is reassuring to find that the ideas which we support are not unrealistic ideals, but have been translated into practice by people working in similar circumstances to ourselves. It is helpful to have access to these ideas and practices and have the opportunity to think through the implications of them for our own practice as individuals and as teams responsible for a course. If such development is to have an impact on institutions and departments rather than on a few individuals, it is desirable for it to be conducted in situ with participation from many of those involved in teaching in a particular area.

The main difficulty in practice may be the potential threat which self-directed learning poses to some teachers. The teacher's role shifts in emphasis away from that of source and controller of learning to that of resource and facilitator. In our experience this is a highly satisfying shift in that it enables us to spent more time on thinking about student learning and less on how to present information. Far from leading us away from the fields of knowledge in which we are interested, it has given us new, and wider, perspectives on them as we see them through many other eyes.

Acknowledgements

We would like to thank Lee Andresen, Ruth Cohen, and John McKenzie for their helpful comments in the preparation of this paper.

REFERENCES

Bawden R (1985) Problem-based learning: An Australian perspective, in Boud D (Ed) Problem-Based Learning in Education for the Professions, Higher Education Research and Development Society of Australasia, Sydney, 43-57

Biggs J B (1982) Student motivation and study strategies in university and college of advanced education populations,Higher Education Research and Development, 1, 33-55

Biggs J B (1986) Enhancing learning skills: the role of metacognition, in Bowden J A (Ed) Student Learning: Research into Practice - The Marysville Symposium, Centre for the Study of Higher Education, The University of Melbourne, Parkville

Boud D J (1988) Moving towards autonomy, in Boud D J (Ed) Developing Student

Autonomy in Learning, Second Edition, London: Kogan Page, 17-39

Boud D J (1989) The role of self-assessment in student grading, Assessment and Evaluation in Higher Education, 14, 1, 20-30

Boud D J (1991) Implementing Student Self-Assessment, Second Edition, Higher Education Research and Development Society of Australasia, Sydney

Boud D J (1992) The use of self-assessment schedules in negotiating learning, Studies in Higher Education, 17,2, 185-200

Boud D J and Feletti G (Eds)(1991) The Challenge of Problem-Based Learning, London: Kogan Page.

Boud D J, Dunn J G and Hegarty-Hazel E H (1986) Teaching in Laboratories, Milton Keynes: Society for Research into Higher Education and Open University Press

Boud D J, Keogh R and Walker D (Eds)(1985) Reflection: Turning Experience into Learning, London: Kogan Page

Brookfield S D (1982) Independent adult learning. Adults, Psychological and Educational Perspectives No 7. Nottingham, Department of Adult Education, University of Nottingham

Brookfield SD (1986) Understanding and facilitating adult learning, San Francisco, Jossey-Bass.

Candy P (1987) Evolution, revolution or devolution: Increasing learner-control in the instructional setting, in Boud D and Griffin V (Eds), Appreciating Adults Learning: From the Learners' Perspective, London: Kogan Page

Candy P (1988a) Key issues for research in self-directed learning, Studies in Continuing Education, 10, 104-124

Candy P (1988b) On the attainment of subject-matter autonomy, in Boud D (Ed) Developing Student Autonomy in Learning, Second Edition, London: Kogan Page, 59-76

Cornwall M (1988) Putting it into practice: Promoting independent learning in a traditional institution, in Boud D (Ed) Developing Student Autonomy in Learning, Second Edition, London: Kogan Page, 59-76

Eizenberg N (1986) Applying student learning research to practice, in Bowden J A (Ed) Student Learning: Research into Practice - The Marysville Symposium, Centre for the Study of Higher Education, The University of Melbourne, Parkville

Elton L R B (1982) Assessment for learning, in Bligh D (Ed) Professionalism and Flexibility in Learning, Guildford: Society for Research into Higher Education

Entwistle N J (1981) Styles of Learning and Teaching, London: John Wiley & Sons

Entwistle N J, Hanley M and Hounsell D J (1979) Identifying distinctive approaches to studying, Higher Education, 8, 365-380

Entwistle N J and Ramsden P (1983) Understanding Student Learning, London: Croom Helm

Ferrier B, Marrin M and Seidman J (1988) Student autonomy in learning medicine:

Some participants' experiences, in Boud D J (Ed) <u>Developing Student Autonomy in Learning</u>, Second Edition, London: Kogan Page, 17-39

Fullan M (1982) <u>The Meaning of Educational Change</u>, Toronto: OISE Press

Gibbs G (1981) <u>Teaching Students to Learn: A Student-Centred Approach</u>, The Open University Press, Milton Keynes

Griffith G (1987) Images of interdependence: authority and power in teaching/learning, in Boud D & Griffin V (Eds) <u>Appreciating Adults Learning: From the Learners' Perspective</u>, London: Kogan Page

Harris R (1989) Reflections on self-directed adult learning: Some implications for educators of adults, <u>Studies in Continuing Education</u>, 11, 102-116

Havelock R G (1973) <u>The Change Agent's Guide to Innovation in Education</u>, Englewood Cliffs: Educational Technology Publications

Heron J (1988) Assessment revisited, in Boud D (Ed) <u>Developing Student Autonomy in Learning</u>, Second Edition, London: Kogan Page, 77-90

Heron J (1989) <u>The Facilitators' Handbook</u>, London: Kogan Page

Higgs J (1988) Planning learning experiences to promote autonomous learning, in Boud D (Ed) <u>Developing Student Autonomy in Learning</u>, Second Edition, London: Kogan Page, 40-58

Higgs J (1989) <u>Programme structure and self direction in independent learning programmes</u>, Unpublished PhD Thesis, University of New South Wales, Sydney

Jones J (1990) Reflections upon the undergraduate curriculum, in Moses I <u>Higher Education in the late twentieth century: Reflections on a Changing System - A Festschrift for Ernest Roe</u>, Sydney: Higher Education Research and Development Society of Australasia

Jones J and Putterill M (1988) <u>The quality of university learning environments: A case-study with stage 1 commerce students</u>, Auckland: HERO, University of Auckland

Jones J, Caird K and Putterill M (1989) First year university commence students' views on their environments, <u>Research and Development in Higher Education</u>, 10, 86-97

Knowles M S (1970) <u>The Modern Practice of Adult Education: Androgogy versus Pedagogy</u>, Chicago: Follett Publishing Company

Knowles M S (1975) <u>Self-Directed Learning: A Guide for Learners and Teachers</u>, New York: Association Press

Martin E and Ramsden P (1986) Do learning skills courses improve student learning? in Bowden J A (Ed.) <u>Student Learning: Research into Practice - The Marysville Symposium</u>, Centre for the Study of Higher Education, The University of Melbourne, Parkville

Marton F and Saljo R (1976) On qualitative differences in learning II - Outcome as a function of the learner's conception of the task <u>British Journal of Educational Psychology</u>, 46, 115-127

Newble D I and Jaeger K (1983) The effect of assessments and examinations on the learning of medical students, Medical Education, 17, 165-171

Novak J D and Gowin D B (1984) Learning How to Learn, Cambridge: Cambridge University Press

Parlett M R (1970) The syllabus-bound student, in Hudson L (Ed) The Ecology of Human Intelligence, Harmondsworth: Penguin Books, 272-283

Pask G (1976) Styles and strategies of learning, British Journal of Educational Psychology, 46, 128-148

Perry W G (1970) Forms of Intellectual and Ethical Development in the College Years: A Scheme, New York: Holt, Rinehart and Winston

Ramsden P (1984) The context of learning, in Marton F, Hounsell D and Entwistle N (Eds), The Experience of Learning, Edinburgh: Scottish Academic Press, 144-164

Ramsden P (1988) Studying learning: Improving teaching, in Ramsden P (Ed) Improving Learning: New Perspectives, London: Kogan Page

Rogers C R (1969) Freedom to Learn: A view of what education might become, Columbus: Charles E. Merrill

Rowntree D (1977) Assessing Students: How Do We Know Them?, London: Harper and Row

Schön D A (1987) Educating the Reflective Practitioner, San Francisco: Jossey-Bass

Smith R M (1983) Learning How to Learn: Applied Theory for Adults, Milton Keynes: Open University Press

Stephenson J (1988) The experience of independent study at North East London Polytechnic, in Boud D J (Ed) Developing Student Autonomy in Learning, Second Edition, London: Kogan Page, 17-39

Taylor M (1987) Self-directed learning: more than meets the observer's eye, in Boud D and Griffin V (Eds) Appreciating Adults Learning: From the Learners' Perspective, London: Kogan Page, 179-196

Tompkins C and McGraw M (1988) The negotiated learning contract, in Boud D J (Ed) Developing Student Autonomy in Learning, Second Edition, London: Kogan Page, 17-39

Tough A M (1978) Major learning efforts: Recent research and future directions. Adult Education, 28, 250-263

Tough A M (1979) The Adult's Learning Projects: A fresh approach to theory and practice in adult learning, Toronto: Ontario Institute for Studies in Education

Wilson J D (1981) Student Learning in Higher Education, London: Croom Helm

Witkin H A, Moore C A, Goodenough D R and Cox P W (1977) Field-dependent and field-independent cognitive styles and their educational implications, Review of Education Research, 47, 1-64

CHAPTER 18

LEARNER-MANAGED-LEARNING THROUGH LEARNING WHILE EARNING

By

NORMAN EVANS

Introduction

Learning while earning is a particular version of learner-managed-learning. Quite simply it is a scheme enabling those in full time or part time employment to obtain academic credit for what they have learned or can learn through their day to day employment without being required to attend a formal education institution. There are several essential facilities which need to be available for learning while earning to provide a thoroughly learner centred and controlled mode of academic work. First a particular form of credit accumulation system must be available. Next there must be some academic procedures for negotiating an individual programme of study. Those are essential to meeting the purpose of learner-managed-learning. Two other facilities extend both the possibilities and scope of learner-managed-learning. They are some academic procedures for evaluating, validating and assigning academic credit to any company in-house education and training programmes which may meet the requisite criteria. And last and perhaps of most significance of all, academic provision for the assessment of prior and experiential learning.

The need for credit accumulation

The kind of credit accumulation system which is a prerequisite for making learning while earning available as a version of learner-managed-learning has to be based on the recognition that in contemporary technological societies there many ways in which individual men and women can learn and only some of these are the preserve of academic institutions. To some extent this has always been the case. In the span of human history the hegemony of formal education for entire populations will be seen to have been relatively short lived.We are entering an age when it is possible to buy or hire software learning programmes on a wide range of topics and to use them at home on personal computers.There are therefore a variety of learning systems in addition to what is formally offered in the world of academic learning. This is underlined by the steady expansion of learning facilities offered by companies to their employees to enable these to become more productive and hence beneficial to the companies concerned.It may be argued that unless company employees and management continue to learn, over time the company may fail and the employees will be out of work. Just staying on top of one's job involves a continual process of learning.

Thus a credit accumulation system which can facilitate learning while earning needs to be based on ways of according recognition for learning attainments, irrespective of how these were reached, always provided that the attainment meets certain academic criteria.Such a system is founded on the acceptance of the fact that people may learn many things without going near a university or college, and that the role of academic institutions may extend beyond teaching and research to one of evaluating knowledge and skills acquired in a variety of contexts. Such a system must be underpinned by assessment and quality assurance procedures which preserve the integrity of academic awards.But there is no problem intrinsic to credit accumulation in using procedures similar to those used within institutions for processing academic qualifications; boards of study for approving learning programmes,examining boards for dealing with marks, external examiners to guarantee standards, all need to be established as part of the arrangements for credit accumulation.Such a system of credit accumulation should also be capable of encompassing learning acquired in different educational institutions as well as learning acquired in work situations.

Seen from the point of view of the learner, the learner-managed-learning idea begins to have some force for those in employment who, for whatever reason, wish to obtain some academic award. It involves recording all evidence of learning already acquired in relation to the target qualification being considered. First, all courses already followed and qualifications gained need to be listed. Next come any company in-house courses which have been validated and given credit ratings. Last comes the experiential learning obtained while working which can be scrutinized to see how much can be considered for credit. This is the first stage of the negotiation; the next stage is that of working out a learning programme designed to take the learner employee further along the line to the desired qualification.

Negotiating a programme of study

The main feature of this stage of the negotiation for learning while earning is that it is tripartite; it is between the learner, the employer and the academic and his institution.Of these the key negotiator is the employer since it is he who will be asked to pay for or at least contribute to, the Learning Agreement, as well as be asked for some remission of time so that the employee-learner can undertake some his/her learning off the job.Such an employer needs to be convinced that the cost to the business will bring back benefits of some sort. Further, since in many countries today, the cost of higher and further education is shared between the employers and the state, it is important that the employer sees himself or herself as an equal partner in the negotiation of learning agreements. For the employee, negotiations need to begin by considering his/her day to day work and then move on to what the employer would find valuable for the employee to learn. This should be acceptable to the employee since it points to the development of personal knowledge and skills and to some form of career advancement.Nevertheless such a programme of study must be agreeable both to the learner and to the institution whose award will sanction the programme.

The results of the negotiations need to be set down in a clear fourfold form covering:what is to be learned, how it is to be learned, how the learning is to be assessed and what kind of evidence is to be used to assess what has been learned. Thus all three parties to the process understand and accept the programme of study to be undertaken. It also makes it easier for the academic who will supervise the study to provide support, advice and help, and for the learner to focus sharply on the target and keep on eye on the schedule of study.

Learning agreements should be capable of re-negotiation. However carefully the learning agreement may have been negotiated there are always liable to be unpredictable changes in the life of the learner, which mean that the terms of the agreement cannot be met as planned. A change of function at work; a move to a different part of the country; promotion ; changes in home circumstances such as the birth of a baby, family illness, moving house; all these may individually be disruptive to the best laid plans for study. It is thus important that a learning agreement be capable of being re-negotiated. In this way the learner stays in charge and able to control the rhythm of learning according to what is most appropriate at a particular time. Even without change of personal circumstances it may turn out that the additional learning conscientiously undertaken turns out to be too onerous for the learner. There is also the psychological advantage that the learner stays in charge of his/her own learning and need not be weighed down by the possible anxiety of not being able to keep up with the inexorable pressure of assignments. In its place comes a feeling of personal responsibility which can be a powerful motivator.

Evaluating, validating and assigning credits

The decision as to the number of credits to be awarded for work done is no so easily handled within the idea of learner-managed-learning.The learner naturally wants to know precisely what credits he may obtain for what he already knows or can do. In one sense planning the learning programme is impossible without an acceptance of what is already known. Yet the critical academic issue is the relationship between what may be creditable from the past and the intended learning in the future. It may be that some of the learning from the past which is creditable in academic terms, cannot be credited towards an academic award because it does not fit into the overall learning plan for the award being sought. This can lead to some frustration on the part of the learner unless the position is made absolutely clear at the outset.

Assuming these hurdles are cleared, the next issue concerns the learning agreement itself. Again the learner naturally wants to know just how many credits will be due once the additional study plan has been completed. There can be no absolute answer to that question, but it is the responsibility of the academic authority to give the best indication possible assuming the work is satisfactorily completed. Such work would normally generate a number of credits calculated from the rubric of the credit accumulation scheme, which, in turn reflects the proportion of a full time year of study represented by the content of the learning agreement. It also needs to be considered as being at a particular level, for example at year 1 or 2 or 3 of a bachelor's degree, or as part of a master's degree. At best this can only be a broad indication of how credits are granted, The possibility of re-negotiation introduces further complications into the equation. But as much reassurance as possible must be given to the learner involved who will no doubt have made a considerable commitment to the scheme.

The commitment of the employer is also vital and this needs to go beyond the original negotiation. Line managers and supervisors have a key role to play; indeed it is clear that the success of a learning agreement is often governed by the interest and support shown by the learner's immediate superior. Without that kind of commitment, the learner might be in for a hard time.

Benefits of learner-manged-learning while earning

In principle all should gain from such learning agreements.For the individual learners, having a say in what they want to learn is almost a condition of effective learning; add to this the student paced aspect of the learning agreement plus the possibility of gaining benefit from what has been learned in the past, then the opportunity of obtaining a qualification in this way seems particularly attractive.

For employers, the benefits are not negligible. First to have employees who are keen to enhance their skills and knowledge is an asset.Secondly, there may be direct financial gains in so far as employees who subscribe to learning agreements may cut down their total attendance at Further Education classes which employers may have been paying for. Thirdly and more significantly, the scheme may help the recruitment and retention of key members of staff who are attracted by the staff development and career prospect aspect of learning agreements. For academic institutions there are also a number of benefits.Recruiting relatively older members of the population will add to student numbers at a time when finance to educational institutions is largely determined by numbers on roll. Although some students might enrol for necessary supplementary courses, much of the enrolment will probably be for the supervision of projects or the devising of programmes of study. Learning agreements as a version of learner-managed-learning are not an untried experiment. The Learning From Experience Trust which pioneered these schemes, began with Jaguar Cars, Wimpy International, JBS Computer Services Ltd and the Training Agency of the Department of Employment. Learning agreements are being used increasingly across a wide range of companies and occupations.

Problems perceived by employers and academics

Unfortunately most employers and many educational institutions are unfamiliar with the scheme or sceptical about its merits. Most employers have either progressed through the formal education system or have a clear idea as what higher education means in terms of three or four year full-time courses, or as a rather poor second best, part-time study for two or three evenings a week for four or five years. It takes time for them to assimilate the implications of an entirely different style of higher education represented by credit accumulation, the validation of a company's in-house courses and the assessment of prior experiential learning. Even when they have been given a careful account of how the alternative system works, they remain cautious about adopting learning agreements for their employees. Many management issues arise. Which grades or categories of employees would best be served by learning agreements? In practice they can apply to all categories. What time and therefore resource commitments are implied in having line managers and supervisors involved? In fact the involvement of supervisory staff can lead to staff development activities for such staff. How would learning agreements fit in with staff appraisal? Is there a danger that, offering these opportunities to staff, they might move elsewhere equipped with better qualifications? This, of course, is a general problem not specific to this form of staff development. What are the costs of having an academic institution providing the essential services of negotiation, supervision and assessment? The best way of considering this question is to think in terms of the alternative costs of hiring academic services on a consultancy basis. The company may also query the quality and standing of the awards achieved. Strictly these ought not to be any different from any other award provided by the collaborating institution.

This last question is one which is also of great importance to academics who validate these awards. From the academics' viewpoint what matters is the coherence of a set of credits derived from a variety of different sources and representing differing pieces of work. Further, the reliability and validity of the assessment procedures must be beyond reproach and stand up to the same tests as those used for more traditional examinations. Academic institutions have devised a set of procedures encoded in regulations which are buttressed by case law which enable them to deal with such problems. But clearly each case needs to be argued on its merits, and although negotiations and adjustments will occur, the ultimate judge of whether or not a learning agreement is appropriate for a particular award lies with the validating body. Just as employers may be sceptical at first and take time to accept the benefits of the scheme, so educational institutions may not be enthusiastic about such a scheme. They may wonder how far such work should be central to their activities or merely peripheral.Even individual learners may prefer the perceived safety of a well tried traditional course to the experimental and untried learner managed work-related course. But as explained earlier, learner-managed-learning through work-based learning agreements should ultimately prove very attractive to employees, employers and educational institutions.

CHAPTER 19

LEARNER-MANAGED-LEARNING:AN ANDROGOGIC POLICY FOR HIGHER EDUCATION?

By

Gerald T Fowler

Introduction

We live in a small and shrinking world where ideas spread across the globe more rapidly than ever before in human history. It is therefore not surprising that the concept of Learner-Managed- Learning is now becoming increasing acceptable in many countries. It is imperative therefore that we share our experience, learn from each other, and above all define more precisely what we mean by Learner-Managed-Learning. Of course, the self-same concept, or a very similar one, may masquerade under several different names, but there is a core of ideas underlying the concept which transcends all nomenclature.

Characteristics of Learner-Managed-Learning(LML)

It seems to me that some or all of the following elements are central to Learner-Managed-Learning.

1)   The learner either wholly or partly designs his or her own programme to meet his or her own needs. It goes without saying that this will normally be done with guidance from counsellors and from discipline specialists, but the part played by the learner is essential. It equally goes without saying that where LML is designed to achieve a qualification, or credit towards a qualification (which may be transferable between institutions), it is vital that there be a framework which makes the assessment of achievement and determination of credit possible. This does not alter the centrality of the learner. In this respect the concept of LML has much in common with the Illichian notion of "deschooling"(Illich,1971).

2)   The learner nevertheless has access to necessarily "institution-alised" resources, both physical and human. The environment for successful learning, especially in equipment-intensive areas of study, may not exist in the wider community, or if it does, may not be readily accessible. Nevertheless, the learner also has access to that wider community and may rely upon institutional resources to help him or her to systematise what (s)he learns in that wider

environment. This overcomes one weakness in Illich's mere Register of Scholars and Students, where the scholars as well as the students may not have ready access to such resources.

3)   The learner monitors his or her own progress, alone or with peers and/or with counsellors. Learner-Managed-Learning does not mean that the learner is cast adrift on the ocean of knowledge with no pilot and no compass.

4)   The learner similarly shares in the assessment of his or her own achievements. Only in this way can the personal self-awareness of the learner be enhanced. The difficulty with traditional methods of examining the results of a student's endeavours is that the results often seem to be handed down from on high, with little explanation of how marks were determined, and with consequent puzzlement on the part of the learner.

5)   The learner's programme may cross "academic" or disciplinary boundaries. Most of us accept today the notion that the divisions we impose upon human knowledge are a form of social construction, not only to protect the standing and hierarchy of (to others) arcane expertise, but also to permit the readier comprehension by the feeble human mind of the vast diversity of nature and of art. A synthesis of elements drawn from more than one discipline may thus lead to new perceptions, and may contribute to the development of new skills. Here I need only draw attention to the work of Professor Basil Bernstein(1971,1973) and to that of Michael F D Young(1971,1977).

Self-development and Learner-Managed-Learning
To much Learner-Managed-Learning the concept of self-development on the basis of the learner's own experience is central, for it is the desire to systematise that experience and to draw on it to gain new perceptions and new skills which provides the motivation for the learner to undertake further study. Such self-development demands:

1)   The recognition of the value of experiential as opposed to formal learning. It is obvious after a moment's thought that human beings learn far more, both about the world and about themselves, through their day-to-day experiences, whether at the workplace or at home or in the community, than they ever do in the classroom. Of course, it is often what they have learnt in the classroom that enables them to make sense of, and to order, that experience. Nevertheless we have within education systems acted as if formal learning were alone of value and that achievements within formal learning were alone measurable. There is little doubt that this has contributed both to social stratification, and to the neglect of talent.

2) It follows that in LML we must encourage the learner to draw upon his own experientially acquired knowledge and skills, and indeed to develop that experience as part of the process of study. That cannot be achieved unless account is taken in the assessment of the learner, both prior to the period in which (s)he undertakes a period of LML and at its completion, of what has been learnt through experience and what use has been made of it. It remains more difficult to assess experientially acquired knowledge and skills than to assess those learnt as part of a formal curriculum simply because, in the latter form of learning, the objective is to master a corpus of knowledge which is predetermined. It is nevertheless not impossible, and enough work has now been done in many countries, notably the USA, for us to continue to develop relatively sophisticated methods of assessing experiential learning.

3) Self-development also demands the encouragement of self-reliance. It remains all too common for those who left formal education at a relatively early age to defer to the wisdom and judgement of those with superior academic qualifications, even if these latter have had relatively little experience, and have profited even less from that which they have had. That is why it is so important in LML that the student should make use of his or her own assessment of need, and of his or her own assessment of achievement. Self-reliance thus entails self-scrutiny and the exercise of responsibility.

4) There must equally be a recognition that <u>certain</u> capabilities have always been acquired, and perhaps have to be, largely through doing. For example we all recognise that teachers must be trained and that practice, i.e. experience, is an essential part of the process of developing a good teacher. Even more strikingly, there has been in the post-war years a massive growth in the number of courses in Management, so much so that one begins to wonder how the early entrepreneurs of the industrial revolution ever managed anything at all, for they knew nothing of Management Theory. In fact, one does not have to believe that good managers are made in heaven alone to accept that it is the kicks and rewards of running enterprises, even educational enterprises, which are the best tutor to the budding manager.

5) None of this is revolutionary <u>per se</u>. In practice we all learn and develop in this way. My own career is an odd example, since in the early part of it I taught Ancient History in the almost equally ancient University of Oxford; yet via many twists and turns, including a period in politics for part of which I was responsible for the guidance and restructuring of industry, I became the Rector of a relatively modern

Polytechnic devoted to the development of innovative courses, new modes of learning, and offering a wide variety of vocationally-oriented courses, rather than the development of pure theory. An even better example is Margaret Thatcher, who began her career as a research chemist, became a tax lawyer, had ministerial experience in Her Majesty's Treasury and in running the education system of the country, and ended up as Prime Minister of the United Kingdom. Some might argue that one or both of us has learnt the wrong things from our experience, but it is incontestible that we have learnt something. What is revolutionary is the formal recognition of this fact educationally and academically.

Learner-Managed-Learning and assessment

On the one hand, in programmes of LML leading to a qualification or educational award, this might be described as "coming to terms with credentialism", and wilder spirits may see that as undesirable. But on the other, it is necessary that the wider world, not least that of employment, should have some ready means of assessing achievement which is comprehensible to them as well as to us. In any event, the formal recognition of what has been learnt by experience, and of what one can do as well as what one knows within a defined sphere, is vital to building self-confidence in the individual, and hence to enterprise.

Peer-group working and assessment are essential to building cooperation and team-working, and hence, are of the essence of Learner-Managed-Learning. We may contrast here the narrow goals and the rivalry encouraged by some traditional academic courses, which may ultimately lead to what verges on solipsism. There the ambition is to be "top of the class" - or the class-list. Yet while modern economies in almost all aspects of their operation, from technological innovation through marketing to the delivery of health or social services, depend upon enterprise, they also depend upon the ability to work within a team. This feature of LML therefore conduces to the view that it is not only well-suited to the personal development of the individual, but is also, in the context of the late twentieth century, economically efficient and desirable. It does not, of course, fit easily with the view sometimes expressed by right-wing politicians that there is no society, but only individuals and family. But then most collective enterprises do not fit easily into that philosophy either.

Learner-Managed-Learning: an androgogical model for higher education

The University of East London has tried to give a lead in British higher education to the development of LML. It has an MSc (Management) by Self-Managed Learning. This contains an element of peer-group work alongside individual work. It also relies heavily on peer-group assessment. A few students do not fit readily with this pattern of working. One case of appeal is known to me, against the result of peer-group assessment. But in general the course seems to have been a success.

Much more important, not least in terms of numbers, is the programme of Independent Study. Here we have had in any one year over 900 students, full-time, and part-time, on a programme which is unique in the United Kingdom. As with any well-managed programme of LML, students are encouraged to progress from one stage to the next so that there are several stopping-off points in the whole programme. A student may enrol for a Diploma of Higher Education, and if successful proceed to a Degree. Other students enrol for the full three-year Degree programme at the outset. Successful students may thereafter proceed to a Masters degree, whether an MA or an MSc. The programme embodies self-design, with guidance, of the course to be followed by each learner, which may embody a very large element of practical or creative work. There is, within broad parameters, self-design by each learner of the modes of assessment which shall apply, and the balance between them. Guidance is provided, alongside specialist tuition. There is access to the whole institution, and to the wider community. Standards are assured not only by External Examiners, but also by an Assessment Board, which vets each learner's programme before (s)he undertakes it. Other institutions in Britain and elsewhere have experimented with this model as indicated by the authors of other chapters in this book.

Finally, if one accepts the philosophy of Recurrent Education, it seems to me that LML is the only possible model for the development of much of higher education. Technological and social change occur at an ever more rapid pace. They necessitate for most if not all, a return to formal or semi-formal learning, or to semi-formal learning running in parallel with work, at several points in a normal working life. The adult learner must be self-motivated, and will normally seek to build on his or her experience hitherto. Since the experience and the needs of each will differ from that of any other, each must have a very strong part in the design of a learning programme, and in the assessment of achievement upon its completion. Each will want credit for that achievement which can be recorded and can accumulate. Only LML can fully meet these requirements. LML is thus not a fad of the late twentieth century, but a major paradigm for the development of higher education in the twenty-first century.

REFERENCES

Bernstein B(1971), <u>Class, Codes and Control</u>, RKP; and (1973) Paladin; and numerous other writings

Illich I D(1971) <u>Deschooling Society</u>, Harper and Row

Illich I D(1974) <u>After Deschooling, What?</u>, Writers and Readers Publishing Cooperative

Young M F D(Ed)(1971) <u>Knowledge and Control</u>, Collier-Macmillan

Young M F and Whitty G(Ed)(1977) <u>Society, State and Schooling</u>, The Falmer Press

CHAPTER 20

FAITH IN LEARNER-MANAGED-LEARNING

By

EUNICE HINDS

In a Learner-Managed-Learning Conference, by experiencing the process ourselves and participating in discussions which clarify the issues, we are able to see how this educational initiative can be of value to a new development such as the new University of Silesia.The subtitle of the Opava conference was ENTERPRISING STUDENTS FOR ENTERPRISING SOCIETIES, I want to make it quite clear that the word enterprise does not just refer to making money, but to making things happen. The conference is, itself an example of enterprise; a small group of people had the vision to see the possibilities and the confidence in that vision to use their enterprise and make this conference happen.

Enterprise is relevant to people working in politics or community projects. It is relevant to people working to build a new university. The quality of enterprise which LML builds is such that students will gain confidence in themselves and the competence to make things happen.

Learner-Managed-Learning is about having confidence and competence. It is about individuals believing that they are able to change things, that they can be enterprising and can make things happen. Too often education emphasises what the student does not know or cannot do rather than building on capabilities and improving performance.

In Learner-Managed-Learning we are aiming to give the student confidence in their own ability, to show them that they can do things and that what they do not yet know can be learnt. We are aiming to motivate the student to believe they can achieve and become enterprising individuals who can make things happen. When I used to teach on Management courses I used to use the example of two spirals. The first is positive in that the spiral is `I can, I will, I do' while the second is negative `I can't, I won't, I don't'. What L.M.L. is aiming to do is to get students onto the positive spiral.

Of course there will be setbacks. Sometimes things that seem positive at one point will later appear as less successful. One of my earlier achievements was to lead the protests against the South African Government when it seemed possible that Nelson Mandela would be hanged. As a result of the international protests the decision was taken to imprison rather than hang Mr Mandela. I felt euphoric at this success and for years saw it as an example of what I could achieve. I used it when people said I was wasting my time by political involvement and couldn't achieve anything. It was my example of `enterprise' that could make things happen.

Gradually the years went by and I began to think that this great success had, in fact, probably been a failure. I began to see that a person spending a life in prison could be intolerable; that it may be a worse sentence than death. Gradually I started to move to the negative spiral, thinking that achievement was impossible.. Recently I have come back to the positive spiral, feeling that the life was worth saving, the release of Nelson Mandela and recent events in South Africa have obviously influenced this. What I want to emphasise is that it is important to re-examine our position, to be reflective practitioners. It is necessary to analyze successes and failures.

For me, the Opava conference was a success; I feel that I succeeded in bringing about the meeting against the odds of poor physical communication, difficult logistics and financial uncertainty. I had confidence, and I hope some competence and I made it happen. It is part of being prepared to take risks because of personal faith in ones own ability to cope with the unknown. If one only ever deals with the totally familiar one never proceeds to the level of being able to perform more than the minimum. One is never enterprising and there is no development.

I am very pleased that the conference did happen at the time when a new university was being launched. I was delighted when we witnessed the local council donating a building for the university. However, I want to say, very clearly that buildings do not make an institution a success. It is the people who make an institution. If our participation at this conference has given those present from the new university the confidence to take the risk of trusting their students, then something of massive value will have been achieved.

If the conference gives all of us the confidence to return to our own work situation and take risks to allow new developments, then we will be well on the way to be enabling our students to learn in a way that enables them to build up their own competencies. Have we the confidence in ourselves to allow the students to challenge traditional subject boundaries? Dare we step outside our area of expert knowledge and admit that in some situations the student, because of life experience, may know more than we do? The students almost certainly knows more about what motivation is relevant and about what suit their particular needs. Can we change our competence from that of the subject specialist to that of the facilitator of student learning and autonomy?

Subject areas change so quickly that it is almost impossible to keep totally up to date, we can not know what will be the relevant information or factual knowledge which will be necessary in ten or fifteen years time.

If we cannot know, we cannot teach the information to the students. What we can teach them is how to find the information. We can teach them to be lifelong autonomous learners. We can motivate them so that they have the confidence to do things and the competence to find the right information or follow the right process. In other words we are aiming to make students entrepreneurs of their own learning. Learner-Managed-Learning is about giving students confidence and competence so that they are enterprising students for enterprising societies.

INDEX